*Reflections of an
Unconverted Convert*

Reflections *of an* Unconverted Convert

Elie Wiesel, the Problem of God,
and One Jew's Return Home

Murray Joseph Haar

FOREWORD BY
Steven Leonard Jacobs

CASCADE *Books* • Eugene, Oregon

REFLECTIONS OF AN UNCONVERTED CONVERT
Elie Wiesel, the Problem of God, and One Jew's Return Home

Copyright © 2022 Murray Joseph Haar. All rights reserved. Except for brief quotations in critical publications or reviews, no part of this book may be reproduced in any manner without prior written permission from the publisher. Write: Permissions, Wipf and Stock Publishers, 199 W. 8th Ave., Suite 3, Eugene, OR 97401.

Cascade Books
An Imprint of Wipf and Stock Publishers
199 W. 8th Ave., Suite 3
Eugene, OR 97401

www.wipfandstock.com

PAPERBACK ISBN: 978-1-6667-3056-2
HARDCOVER ISBN: 978-1-6667-2224-6
EBOOK ISBN: 978-1-6667-2225-3

Cataloguing-in-Publication data:

Names: Haar, Murray Joseph, author. | Jacobs, Steven Leonard, foreword.

Title: Reflections of an unconverted convert : Elie Wiesel, the problem of God, and one Jew's return home / by Murray Joseph Haar ; foreword by Steven Leonard Jacobs.

Description: Eugene, OR: Cascade Books, 2022 | Includes bibliographical references.

Identifiers: ISBN 978-1-6667-3056-2 (paperback) | ISBN 978-1-6667-2224-6 (hardcover) | ISBN 978-1-6667-2225-3 (ebook)

Subjects: LCSH: Wiesel, Elie, 1928–2016—Religion. | Holocaust (Jewish and Christian theology). | God (Judaism)—History of doctrines. | Providence and government of God—Judaism—History of doctrines.

Classification: BM610 .H30 2022 (print) | BM610 (ebook)

12/09/22

Copyrights received from *Interpretation* for article written in the spring of 1999.

Contents

Foreword by Steven Leonard Jacobs | vii
Acknowledgments | ix

Introduction | 1
Chapter One: Who Was Elie Wiesel and What Did He Say about and to God? | 5
Chapter Two: Israel Laments Its Relationship to God | 10
Chapter Three: God Laments His Relationship with Israel | 27
Chapter Four: The Book of Job and the Holocaust | 36
Chapter Five: Elie Wiesel and the Problem of God: *Night, Ani Maamin*, and *The Trial of God* | 50
Chapter Six: Why God Is a Problem: The Christian Years | 71
Chapter Seven: How Should We Live after Auschwitz? | 85

Afterword | 98
Bibliography | 107

Foreword

Not all of the victims of the event known as the Holocaust were those who experienced and survived the horrors. For some among them, Murray Haar included, they transmitted both their physical and their psychic pain to their children, the so-called "second generation" of victims. While not alone, his moving memoir *Reflections of an Unconverted Convert* may be somewhat unique. For in running away from both the craziness and fire of his family, he embraced another religious tradition, that of Lutheran Christianity, becoming, in the process, not only a Lutheran husband and father, but an ordained pastor and academic as well.

Yet even this embrace could not quiet the haunting of his own identity as well as his intellectual wrestling with the meaning of his former way of life and his present one as well, all deeply affected by the Holocaust journey of his own parents. In his struggle to return to his Jewish roots and Jewish identity, and the support he continued to experience in the most unlikely of places, Murray Haar has much to teach us not only about what it means to be a Jew in the aftermath of the Holocaust, but what it may mean to be a Christian as well.

The questions he asks and the answers he gives which come from the depths his soul, initially in his examination of the biblical community laments as well as the writings of Elie Wiesel, his personal midrash, after Auschwitz, forces us his readers to grapple anew with the meaning of events now more than eighty years old. In doing so, he serves as a very human bridge to dialogue between caring Jews and sensitive Christians who know instinctively that their religious worlds have been irrevocably changed forever.

Above all, his story is one of courage, not only that of his parents and their painful attempt to rebuild their shattered lives to the best of their damaged ability, but his as well. Reflections of an Unconverted Convert thus becomes a tribute to the resilience of the human spirit when confronted with the enormity of events which makes no sense and with horrors which transcend the human imagination.

Where Murray Haar's journey will ultimately lead him as he continues to wrestle with where he has been and where he is remains an open question. One can only hope that he will continue to write and continue to reflect upon that journey so that we, too, may join and learn from him.

Rabbi Steven Leonard Jacobs
Aaron Aronov Chair of Judaic Studies
The University of Alabama

Acknowledgments

Thanks to Augustana University (Sioux Falls) for a one-year sabbatical that gave me time to think, read, and write.

Thanks to my colleagues in the religion department at Augustana for their ongoing support and encouragement throughout the years.

Special thanks to two professors at Augustana with whom I taught an important class ("Light in the Darkness: Courage and Evil in the Twentieth Century") for over twenty years, Drs. Peter Schotten and Sandra Looney.

Thanks to Rev. Steve Wohlfeil for listening to many versions of this book and for our fine discussions over the years. He is a true friend and a mensch.

To my children, Jennifer, Nathan, and Matthew, with love, that they might know why their father traveled the religious road he did.

And the most important thanks to my wise and caring wife, Jill Storm (*ChavaLeah*), my true *ezer knegdo*. I cannot thank her enough for tolerating our many theological and philosophical discussions that helped me to think through my thoughts about the book. With affection, friendship, and love, I dedicate this book to her.

Having said all of that, I bear full responsibility for the contents and character of this book.

Introduction

On November 14, 1979, Elie Wiesel stood in a packed gymnasium on the campus of Augustana College in Sioux Falls, South Dakota, and spoke to students and teachers about "those days." His talk was entitled "Building a Moral Society." I can still hear his powerfully haunting voice saying these words, "In memory lies redemption."[1] He implored us, saying, if we remember what happened in "those days," we may prevent it from happening again. He talked about why he could not give up being a believing and observant Jew. He said, "As a Jew, who am I to say stop? After Abraham, Isaac, Jacob, Rabbi Akiva, Rashi . . . Who am I to say stop?" And he chided us to realize, "We do not begin to transmit our lives through falsehood." And then he said the words that changed my life forever: "A Jew," he said, "should live his life inside his Jewish tradition, a Christian inside his or her Christian tradition. Only in this way can a Jew or Christian achieve universality."

In this moment, Wiesel had revealed to me how I was living my life out of falsehood about myself and about God.

I am a Jew. I left Judaism and became a Christian. After many years I returned to Judaism and the Jewish community. Elie Wiesel played a key role in my return. I grew up in the Bronx, New York, a child of Holocaust survivors, and it was there I first

1. Wiesel, Augustana Lecture.

heard about God. As a boy, I spoke only Yiddish until I was six years old; I attended Yeshiva (a Jewish parochial school) and for a few summers I went to day camp at the local YMHA (Young Men's Hebrew Association). On the bus ride to camp in New Jersey, we sang, "He's got the whole world in his hands . . . He's got this little bus in his hand." Everything that happened, good or bad, was in some way the will of God. My young Jewish faith was precisely that: young, naïve, and simplistic.

My parents were Holocaust survivors. My mother, Pola, escaped the Nazis by running through the Polish forests with her sister to make her way to Russia. My father, Bernard, was a prisoner in Auschwitz as well as various Russian labor camps. My parents met in a German DP (Displaced Persons) camp after the war, married, and came to America in 1947. I was born in 1948. My parents constantly implored me to be a good Jew and a good American. They did not tell me how to do this. And they rarely talked about the Holocaust.

I ran away from that life in 1966, joined the Air Force, converted to Christianity in 1971, became a Christian Lutheran pastor and teacher. I spent too many nights with too little sleep feeling guilt and shame for becoming a Christian. Many years after hearing Elie Wiesel speak and reading his books, I returned to the Jewish religion and community. For the first time in my life, I was at home within my own skin and soul. I was sleeping through the night.

Elie Wiesel was not a theologian eager to talk about God. In all his writings Wiesel does not talk about God. He talks to God. Wiesel grew up in a tradition that not only allowed questioning and accusing God but encouraged such talk as an inherent part of faith. In his first book, *Night*, Wiesel clearly states: "I am the accuser and God the accused."[2]

Wiesel had not stopped believing in God, but he had come to doubt the justice of God. Throughout his writings, Wiesel questions God's methodology, morality, sanity, and most importantly God's commitments to the Jewish people. "Wiesel's experience of

2. Wiesel, *Night*, 79.

INTRODUCTION

theodicy during the Holocaust is exactly *the problem* that perplexes so many post-Holocaust Jews still: Where was God or at least where was the manifestation of God's justice and compassion during the Holocaust? God's apathetic absence haunts Wiesel and the heroes of his works. God observed the Holocaust but did nothing. Time and again Wiesel asserts that the Holocaust was a trial and, in a sense, the death of God."[3] "Wiesel's love of God and his presentation of God's response to the Holocaust are never allowed to obscure that fact of God's apathetic inactivity, nor can they ever absolve God of his guilt. Perhaps someday someone will explain how, on the level of man, Auschwitz was possible; but on the level of God, it will forever remain the most disturbing of mysteries."[4] For Wiesel God remains a problem and there is no answer except faithful defiance. "Elie Wiesel was a religious Jew. Argument and defiance are his ways of expressing faith and hope after Auschwitz."[5]

How and why Elie Wiesel sees God as a problem and can yet think of himself as faithful is the motivation for this book. I have, for the most part, adopted Wiesel's way of approaching God. How can Wiesel speak of God as both dead and alive? In so many ways, I, a Jew whose parents went through a kind of fire, I too wrestle with Wiesel's questions and doubts. The book begins with an examination of Wiesel's Jewish background. What sort of Judaism influenced and effected his approach toward God? How was that Judaism rooted in the Jewish Scriptures and traditions? What parts of the tradition endorsed such questioning? In what ways did Wiesel go beyond the tradition?

While Elie Wiesel was not a systematic theologian, his talking to God opens all sorts of doors for those who care to think about God with honesty, including Jews, Christians, and Muslims. In his writings he disputes any kind of naïve faith that refuses to look at what happened at Auschwitz. For Wiesel, whatever religious persuasion a person holds, that persuasion is compelled to pass through Auschwitz. He asks: what happened to God's

---

3. Laytner, *Arguing with God*, 215.
4. Laytner, *Arguing with God*, 217.
5. Laytner, *Arguing with God*, 222.

promises to the Jewish people after they pass through Auschwitz? And I would add: What happens to Jesus, the Christian creeds, hymns, confessions after they pass through Auschwitz? What happens to the Muslim faith, the Quran, and Muhammad after they pass through Auschwitz? Wiesel's sense is that everything is changed by the experience of Auschwitz, including all religions, all human beings, and of course, God. For Wiesel, if you want to believe in God, you must explain how your faith in God works at Auschwitz. If it works there, it will work anywhere. If it does not work there, what good is it?

How and why was Wiesel able to question and accuse God of wrongdoing and think he was being faithful? And what are the implications for the monotheistic religions after Auschwitz, according to Wiesel? That is, if believers and unbelievers were to take seriously what Wiesel is saying, how might they have to rethink their respective theological positions and faith commitments? What are the limits of Wiesel's theological and religious methodology? Can human beings live with such a tentative and problematic view of their God? Would they be better off and more honest to be atheists or agnostics? Can Wiesel's accusations and questions addressed to God be applicable to any person's religious faith? Should they be?

Chapter One: *Who Was Elie Wiesel and What Did He Say about and to God?*

As far back as I can remember I have been a religious person. I suppose attending the first six years of school at a Yeshiva (Jewish parochial school) proved to be an important impact on my religious beliefs. But it was specifically Elie Wiesel's writings that later in life forced me to ask questions about God and the Holocaust.

In his memoirs Wiesel writes about his relationship to God as a boy: "I sought God everywhere, tracking him, especially to holy places as though he was hidden there . . . I sought him everywhere, the better to love him, to enjoy his gifts, to share his suffering in our exile: in the chapels of tailors, and of shoemakers, in the great synagogue of the rich, and in the Houses of Study where the poor are gathered."[1] Wiesel was exceedingly religious. He was Jewish in the deepest sense of the word. He trusted and prayed diligently seeking the wisdom of God. He had no doubts. As he wrote, "The divine response lay in the human quest for mystery."[2] Wiesel was fascinated by and engaged with Hasidic mystical experiences to understand the ways of God and to convince God to send the Messiah.

---

1. Wiesel, *All Rivers Run to the Sea*, 33.
2. Wiesel, *All Rivers Run to the Sea*, 33.

REFLECTIONS OF AN UNCONVERTED CONVERT

Everything Elie Wiesel wrote in his life was a commentary on his first book, *Night*. The book begins with the young Wiesel talking about his religious life in the Hungarian village of Sighet. Immersed in these mystical and strange ways of understanding God, Wiesel believed in and studied Hasidic texts and Scriptures. He had been taught by Moishe the beadle to pray to God not for answers but to ask God for the right questions. And Wiesel trusted that God and the Jewish people were inextricably connected. He trusted that the fate of God and the fate of the Jewish people were unbreakably and inextricably bound together. While he knew the ways of God were mysterious and inaccessible, Wiesel believed that God was committed to justice, especially justice for the Jewish people. And Wiesel trusted the Messiah would be arriving soon, very soon.

Rooted in the mystical Hasidic tradition, Wiesel never lost his love for that way of being Jewish. His writings have a certain mystical flavor, and his speaking tone was always tinged with a soft mystical demeanor. He was so rooted in this tradition that he would never completely jettison its core trust in God's ultimate fidelity to the Jewish people.

Despite all of that, his experience of Auschwitz caused him to doubt the God he had trusted as a child. His childlike naivete and his religious image of God died in the camps. He saw what there was to see and nothing was the same after that vision.

For Wiesel there was a distinct before and after. And after Auschwitz, nothing was the same. Auschwitz was a revelation. The event revealed the soul of man and the soul of God. And Wiesel saw himself as a messenger and a witness to what he had seen and what it meant. For the first ten years after the war Wiesel kept silent and only then decided to write. He admitted that he was wrong, in those days, to trust that once people heard his tales, the killing would stop. He said, "Can you imagine how naive we were in those days. We thought by telling our stories we could stop the killing."[3]

In the camps, in those days, there were Jews who lost their faith and Jews who kept or even strengthened their faith. Wiesel

---

3. Wiesel, Augustana Lecture.

CHAPTER ONE: WHO WAS ELIE WIESEL?

found himself in the middle. As his childhood faith was dying, he developed a defiant faith that depended on questioning the justice of God.

For Wiesel, questioning God was not an indication of a weakening or declining form of trust. The question addressed to God was an honest expression of continued trust in the form of puzzlement. If one was going to pray to God during the madness of Auschwitz, one was obligated to speak the truth to God. And Wiesel's obsessive refusal to lie was the great strength at the heart of Wiesel's approach to God. Wiesel felt betrayed by God. The evidence was clear. Day after day in the camps he saw with his eyes what the Nazis were doing. And having seen what he had seen, he would not lie to God. Wiesel had experienced the silence of God.

As Wiesel saw it, that silence was a betrayal of the covenants God had made with the Jewish people. Through the Abrahamic, Mosaic, and Davidic covenants God had established a reciprocal relationship with the Jewish people. God had made promises. And Auschwitz called into question the integrity of those promises. This situation created a theological crisis about which Wiesel was unwilling to lie. Wiesel did not doubt the existence of God. He doubted the justice of God and he believed he had the obligation to call the terrible silence of God to account.

But why was it up to Wiesel to write about what had happened? Because he had survived while so many had perished. Wiesel believed he had a moral obligation to put the question to God, in the name of all of those who had been murdered and could no longer speak. He had to become their spokesperson and he had to figure out a way to speak on their behalf. He could not and would not remain indifferent to what he had seen. He refused to lie or rationalize concerning the silence of God. He would write about what he had seen and experienced. In every book he wrote he would search for a way to speak the truth to God and all of us about the revelations emanating from Auschwitz.

And what was the revelation? What did the Holocaust reveal about God and about human beings? For Elie Wiesel, the silence of God during those days was inexcusable. While there were certainly other historical times when Jews were murdered without God's intervention, the Holocaust was an extraordinary, unprecedented, and systematic slaughter of the Jewish people. It included the destruction of a million and a half Jewish children under the age of ten. For Wiesel, the covenants God made with the Jewish people required God to attend to such a terrible, terrifying event. When God did not act, Wiesel felt betrayed, and this betrayal revealed something about the problematic character and morality of God. God was revealed to be unreliable, inconsistent, and unjust. For Wiesel, a person of faith, there was no alternative except to pray to God with honest questions.

In the camps, Elie Wiesel experienced evil of an unprecedented magnitude. This experience revealed the terrible and frightening capacity of human beings to commit monstrous evil on an unimaginable level. Wiesel talked about trying to look into the eyes of the killers to determine if there was any humanity inside of them.

For Wiesel, the problem of God is not whether God exists. Elie Wiesel was not an atheist. He was not an agnostic. The problem is not the love of God. It is not the will of God. The problem is the justice of God. And this problem is brought into undeniable and traumatic vision and relief in the Holocaust.

So, what is my response to Wiesel? To answer that question, I have to tell you a few things. Having been raised as a religious and observant Jew, as a boy I did not realize I was the child of Holocaust survivors until many years later. But I did realize something terrible had happened because something was amiss in that apartment in the Bronx; my parents were not well. They had emigrated to America after meeting in a DP (Displaced Persons) camp in Germany. They were desperate for peace. But peace eluded them. Whatever had happened to them in Europe in those days had hurt them deeply. They lived in a constant state of emotional panic. The smallest event could cause an emotional upheaval and explosion. In that small apartment, there was a certain kind of craziness. They screamed and argued with each other constantly about money, or, I should say, the lack of money. My father worked as

CHAPTER ONE: WHO WAS ELIE WIESEL?

a clothing operator in the garment district of Manhattan. He did not sleep well and as I remember he was always tired. Whatever money he made was insufficient. So, my parents screamed at each other in Yiddish and Polish about money. They did not have a savings account. They lived from paycheck to paycheck. Despite all that, my father looked much younger than he was. I remember telling him when he turned sixty that he looked young. He responded, "Yes, but I feel old."

In that tiny apartment there were rarely any visitors since most of my relatives had been murdered in the Nazi camps. So, there we were, my younger brother, Leo, and I and my parents. I say again, it was a crazy place where there was lots of panic, being hit with a belt, and precious little peace or tranquility. I think my parents loved me and my brother; they provided for us as best they could, but they were not sure how to parent us.

Despite all of that, there is one important, life-changing moment I remember. One morning when I was about fourteen years old, I was standing at the living room table wearing my tefillin and praying the morning prayers. I noticed my father watching me. When I was done with my prayers, he said, "All this religion is very nice, better you should be a mensch." A mensch is a person of character who acts with honor and integrity, and who is not able to idly stand by while others are suffering. My father's words have marked my life and my determination, though not always successful, to try and be a religious person of character.

Amid all of that, I ran away from that apartment and that craziness three times as a boy, finally leaving for good when I was eighteen. I ran away as fast and as far as I could run. I ran away into Christianity until I met Elie Wiesel, who returned me to myself. My running away was not a planned escape. It was a spontaneous panic and fear which caused me to run. My parents had experienced the darkest of human darkness and it frightened me to my core. I ran away because I had to get away. Many years later, my mother asked me why I had tried to run away. I answered, "Ma, it was crazy in this place." She replied, "Yes, I know."

Chapter Two: *Israel Laments Its Relationship to God*

After Elie Wiesel's fateful visit to Augustana in 1979, I became interested in how Wiesel justified questioning God. Until that moment, it had never occurred to me to question God—but when I did my graduate work in the 1980s, I wrote my dissertation about that very thing, focusing specifically on the lament psalms, which are all about questions for God. From the earliest stories in the Jewish Bible, key characters question God. From Abraham to Moses to Hanna, to the psalms of lament to the book of Job, we see arguing with God to be a central part of what it means to be Jewish. But not only that. We see God accepting, encouraging, and engaging in argument with various representatives of the Jewish people. We see God's mind being changed by the quality and persistence of the arguments, of the laments—or rather of the prayers. While Elie Wiesel did not invent the idea of arguing with God, it was clear where he got the idea. He inherited it from the heart and soul of Jewish tradition.

Lament prayers are rooted in the covenants God made with the Jewish people. A covenant is an agreement between two parties involving promises and obligations on the part of both. In the Bible we observe three such covenants made specifically with the Jewish people: the Abrahamic, the Mosaic, and the Davidic. In the

CHAPTER TWO: ISRAEL LAMENTS ITS RELATIONSHIP TO GOD

covenant made with Abraham in the book of Genesis, God promises him and his descendants land, progeny like the stars in the sky, and most importantly that the promise is forever and unconditional. The Mosaic covenant is made with the people Israel through the agency of Moses in the book of Exodus. The covenant declares it was God who rescued the Hebrews from slavery in Egypt and the Jewish people belong to God and God to them. Part of this covenant was the giving of the commandments and the promise: if the Israelites would follow the commandments, they would be blessed. God's blessing seems to be contingent on obedience to the commandments. But the essential thing to remember is this covenant created an unbreakable and inextricable marriage between God and the Jewish people. Finally, in the Davidic covenant, God promises David there will always be a son of David on the throne. This covenant is unconditional and forever. The Hebrews trusted these covenants and believed they were initiated by God and committed God to the Jewish people and the Jewish people to God. The laments were rooted in these covenants linked to the tenacious Jewish faith that both God and Israel had moral obligations to adhere to the covenants. These obligations were irrevocable marital obligations established by the covenants. To modify a Lutheran notion of grace: God loved Israel by grace alone and Israel loved God by grace alone. When either did not adhere to the agreed upon covenants, they each felt free to question and accuse each other. The biblical laments emanated from love and loyalty.

A lament psalm then is a prayer addressed to God in which the person praying is complaining about the activity or inactivity of God on behalf of the community, in this case, the Israelites. This complaining is not about feeling sorry for the self or the community. When a person prays a lament, he or she is concerned about justice as it relates to the covenants.

But why does the lamenting person think such laments will make a difference? It has to do with the origin of the Jewish people and what makes the Jewish people a community. The Jewish people are not only an ethnic community or a religion. They are a tribal community established, so the observant Jews say, and chosen by God. According to Jewish tradition, if your mother is Jewish, you are a member of the community. Among Reform Jews today, if your father is Jewish and you were brought up Jewish you too are a member of the community. Communal prayers originate from the soul of the community. Laments are visceral prayers intended to move God to act. By the way, there are also members of the Jewish community who do not believe in God. But they, too, are members of the community.

Laments have to do with intimacy. Think of a functional ideal marriage. When you marry someone, you marry the light and the darkness of that person. Both elements are part of the mystery of the relationship. The longer you are married the deeper you enter the light and the darkness. The light and the darkness of each partner make up the soul of the relationship. And this is true of God and the Jewish community. But here is the key: the darkness is not necessarily bad or destructive. As in any painting or work of art, the darkness works with the light to create the genius that is the relationship. In a marriage, each partner can be a mystery and a problem for the other, which is why marriage is such a difficult, exciting, crazy adventure. And as in any marriage, there are met and unmet expectations. When expectations are not met, when one of the partners has acted unreliably over a long period of time, there can be arguments and complaints.

When God does not meet Israel's expectations there can be lament prayers. There are individual and communal laments in the Bible. In each case, these prayers exhort God to act like God, meaning to do what needs to be done to achieve justice. The community lament psalms in the Bible illustrate the heart of the lament tradition. The best examples of communal laments in the Psalter can be encountered in Psalms 44, 74, 80, and 83. While there are other examples, these four psalms will do a good job of introducing us to the heart and soul of laments in the Bible and how they serve to question and argue with God.

The underlying beliefs required for any argument with God and inherent in the laments are described in the following themes.[1]

---

1. The themes discussed here are originally from my doctoral dissertation,

CHAPTER TWO: ISRAEL LAMENTS ITS RELATIONSHIP TO GOD

1) *God is the creator of Israel*

In the Bible God is pictured as the one who established Israel. God is the one who gave Israel the land. God is continually pictured as taking care of and loving his people. God commands the Hebrews to constantly pursue justice. This theme finds its most prominent expression through appeals to the past. In Psalm 80:9-11 the metaphor of the vine is used to describe the care with which God first caused Israel to exist. Here is a romantic reminder of how it was when they first met: "You did bring a vine out of Egypt; you did drive the nations out and plant it. You cleared the ground for it; it took deep root and filled the land. The mountains were covered with its shade, the mighty cedars with its branches to the sea, and its shoots to the river." The person praying reminds God: Israel's origins exist because of the acts of God. Israel is God's creation. The psalmist cries out to God. "Turn again, O God of hosts! Look down from heaven, and see; have regard for this vine, the stock which *your* right hand planted" (Ps 80:15). Israel's existence is inextricably tied to the existence of God.

In Psalm 44 a similar appeal to the past occurs. In 44:3-4 the psalmist reminds God, "you with your own hand did drive out the nations but them [Israel] you did plant; you did afflict the peoples, but them you did set free; for not by their own sword did they win the land nor did their own arm give them the victory; but your right hand and your arm, and the light of your countenance; for you delighted in them." God is pictured as one who delights in his people. The creation of Israel was an act of love on God's part. Israel understands itself to be intimately and inextricably connected to God. The lament prayer reminds God the Jewish people are the sheep of his pasture (Ps 74:1), the tribe of his heritage (Ps 74:19), his beloved (Ps 60:7), his servants (Ps 79:2, 10), the flesh of his saints (79:2), his people, the flock of his pasture (79:13), your protected ones (Ps 83:4), your anointed (Ps 89:39). In Psalm 89:18-19 the psalmist declares, "For *you* are the glory of their strength, by *your* favor our horn is exalted. For our shield belongs to the Lord, our king to the

---

"The God-Israel Relationship in the Community Lament Psalms."

holy one of Israel." And Psalm 74:2 calls upon God to "Remember your congregation, which you have possessed since long ago, which you have redeemed to be the tribe of your heritage." What is vital to understand here is that these texts assert how God has tied God's fate to that of this people. The life of Israel and the life of God are intertwined and inextricable. God, the creator of Israel, has tied God's very being irrevocably to this particular people. And for Elie Wiesel, this irrevocability caused him to question God's faithfulness in most of Wiesel's books.

2) The Faithfulness of God

Why would and how could the ancient Hebrews believe they would be able to influence the mysterious ways of God? What made them think God would listen and act according to their arguments?

Remember, Israel believed she existed because God loved her. And this love was greater than any sin the people might commit. God and Israel were in an intimate relationship. Accordingly, Israel felt free to question and argue with God. Was God acting in a loving manner? A fair and just manner? The questions and accusations directed at God are, in essence, appeals to God's love for Israel. The main concern is to remind God of his love for Israel and his commitment to justice.

God is understood as being unable to keep quiet when his beloved is suffering. The fact that God has been silent and has not acted on behalf of his beloved is puzzling and problematic to the psalmist. The lament prayers seek to understand how God can be silent when the one God loves is in pain. God's silence must mean he has forgotten and does not see his people in pain.

Israel raises accusations and questions not against an impersonal silent deity in the sky, but against the one—God—with whom she is in love and who has promised to love her forever. God's fidelity to justice and his love for Israel is in question because God, who has chosen to be intimately related to the people, Israel, has not lived up to God's commitment to care for them. And this commitment is covenantal. God made promises to Israel—and

CHAPTER TWO: ISRAEL LAMENTS ITS RELATIONSHIP TO GOD

God has not kept his side of the covenants. Expectations have not been met. Attention must be paid! Just listen to the way the psalmist goes after God in Psalm 44:14: "You have sold your people for a trifle, demanding no high price for them." As a lover embarrassed by the actions of her beloved, the psalmist declares in vv. 14-15, "You have made us the taunt of our neighbors, the derision and scorn of those about us. You have made us a byword among the nations, a laughingstock among the peoples." Despite the lack of fidelity on God's part, the psalmist asserts in vv. 18-20 Israel's refusal to desert God. "All this has come upon us, though we have not forgotten you, or been false to your covenant; our heart has not turned back, nor have our steps departed from your way." These are not the words of self-righteousness or corporate constitutional innocence. They are the words of Israel's continuing trust in God's love and justice despite the present situation. These are prayers calling on God to act like God!

In a similar vein, the accusatory questions of Psalm 44:24-25 are those of a lover puzzled by the actions of her beloved. These are questions hurled at God despite his ongoing silence and indifference. "Why do you sleep, O Lord . . . Why do you hide your face? Why do you forget our affliction and oppression?" In these prayers the situation is clear. Israel is in pain and she cannot understand the indifference and silence of her God.

In 74:1 the psalmist asks, "Why does your anger smoke against the sheep of your pasture?" The prayer calls upon God to realize that whatever is causing his present silence is insufficient reason to forget his commitment to justice and his love for his people. With a profound radicality the psalmist is asserting that the love of God for his people is so deep it takes precedence over any judgment or punishment the people might deserve. In reading through these psalms, one gets the sense the person praying is determined to make God aware of the contradiction between God's covenant commitments and God's present apparent indifference. Despite the silence of God, the psalmist continues to hope against hope God will yet act like God on behalf of his people.

Psalm 80:5–6 depicts God as the problem. God is reminded of the pain of Israel caused by his present inaction. "O Lord, God of hosts, how long will you be angry with your people's prayers? You have fed them with the bread of tears and given them tears to drink in full measure." In v. 13, the psalmist questions God, "Why then have you broken down its walls, so that all who pass along the way pick its fruit?" With these words Israel pictures herself as the victim of God's indifference and silence.

This emphasis on God as the problem continues in Psalms 83 and 89. In 83:2 God is petitioned, "O God, do not keep silence; do not hold your peace or be still, O God!" In Psalm 89:39–41, the psalmist charges God with violating his intimate relationship to his people as well as its king. "But now you have cast off and rejected, you are full of wrath against your anointed; you have renounced the covenant with your servant . . . You have breached all his walls . . ." And in v. 47 the prayer asks, "How long, O Lord? Will you hide yourself forever? How long will your wrath burn like fire?" And in verse 50, like a deceived lover, the psalmist asks God, "Lord, where is your steadfast love of old which by your faithfulness you promised to David?"

Sometimes we moderns have the impression it was only recently God has become a problem. Atheists today write as if they have newly discovered the problem of God. But in these lament prayers, we can observe that over two thousand years ago God was already a problem. The ancients were aware of the inconsistency, unreliability, and ambiguity of the ways of God. Here we see them praying to God in hopes of understanding God's silence and indifference. The fact is, no matter how some contemporary religious people might try to defend and cover up for the deity, God was a problem then and remains a problem now. Elie Wiesel seemed to be aware of God's inscrutability and problematic methodology and because of this felt free to raise his voice in lament.

CHAPTER TWO: ISRAEL LAMENTS ITS RELATIONSHIP TO GOD

3) Israel in Pain

At the heart of the lament prayers is the belief that if Israel is in pain, God is obligated to respond. This obligation is not merely a covenantal obligation, though that is certainly true. God is obligated to act due to his intimate relationship to Israel. It was believed God could not help but respond to situations in which God's people are suffering.

Where did the Hebrews get such an idea? Why were they convinced God would respond to their cries for help? Their beliefs were rooted in their foundational stories about the exodus from Egypt. Exodus 2:23–25 reads, "And the people of Israel groaned under their bondage, and cried out for help, and their cry under bondage came up to God. And God heard their groaning, and God remembered his covenant with Abraham, with Isaac, and with Jacob. And God saw the people of Israel, and God knew their pain." God intimately knows the pain of the Israelites and is compelled to respond, not only out of covenantal loyalty but also out of empathy and love for his people. Their pain moves God to act.

This faith in God's empathy for Israel's pain is also found in the community lament psalms. Israel exists because God has heard their groaning and has acted on their behalf in the past. Psalm 44:2 asserts the fathers have told the children all God did for the people in the past. And then in 44:25 the psalmist asks God, "Why do you forget our affliction and oppression?" Psalm 79:11 implores God to let the groans of the prisoners come before him and Psalm 80:9–14 recalls the exodus experience while describing the present pain of Israel.

The community lament prayers are not merely motivations employed by the psalmist to get God to act. It goes deeper than that. God is intimate with Israel to the extent that God hears the cries and groans of his people. To the extent God ignores or does not respond to their cries, God is being unfaithful to the God-Israel relationship. Biblical lament prayers are intended to move God to be faithful to the covenants God established and to God's relationship with Israel. For Elie Wiesel it seems to be inconceivable that God could be aware of what Israel was enduring and not be moved to act.

4) The Fate of Israel and the Fate of God

Closely related to the assumption God hears and knows of Israel's pain was the belief the fate of Israel and the fate of God were bound together. The Israelites trusted God had decided to enter human history as a partner with the Jewish people. God had made himself a partner to the fate of the Jewish people, whose historical experiences did not leave God unaffected. In biblical and rabbinic texts again and again, God is pictured as having taken up residence among the Jewish people. The Jewish people is the dwelling place of God. What happens to them happens to God. This inextricable relationship between God and Israel was not seen as an idea manufactured by Israel. The binding together of God and Israel was God's decision to allow God's fate to be connected to a particular people.

The community lament psalms are aware of this theme. Psalm 74:2 calls upon God to "remember your congregation which you have gotten of old, which you have redeemed to be the tribe of your heritage. Remember Mt. Zion, where you have dwelt." This belief that God lived in and with a particular people is evidenced in Psalm 74:4, where the psalmist speaks of the attack by Israel's enemies and says, "Your enemies have roared in the midst of your holy place . . . They set your sanctuary on fire, to the ground they desecrated the dwelling place of your name." In v. 10 the psalmist connects the actions of the enemy with an attack on God. He asks, "How long, O God, is the enemy to scoff? Is the enemy to revile your name forever?" And in v. 18 God is told, "Remember this, O Lord, how the enemy scoffs and an impious people reviles your name." Psalm 74 concludes, "Arise O God, plead your cause; remember how the impious scoff at you all the day. Do not forget the clamor of your enemies, the uproar of your adversaries which goes up continuously." The fact is, that in Israel's lament tradition, an attack upon Israel was seen to be a simultaneous attack on God.

CHAPTER TWO: ISRAEL LAMENTS ITS RELATIONSHIP TO GOD

It was not only the physical attacks on Israel that were seen as affecting God. The verbal taunts of the enemy were also understood as being taunts against God. Psalm 79:12 calls upon God to "return to the bosom of our neighbors the taunts with which they have taunted you, O Lord." The plans of the enemy to destroy Israel are understood as plans directed against God as well. Psalm 80:6 reads, "They conspire with one accord; against you they make a covenant." Look at Psalm 89:51–52: "Remember O Lord. How your servant is scorned, how I bear in my bosom the insults of many peoples, with which your enemies taunt, O Lord, with which they mock the footsteps of your anointed."

Let us be clear. This belief that Israel and therefore God were being simultaneously attacked, i.e., any attack on one meant an attack on the other, was not evidence of Israel's nationalistic or particularistic pride or arrogance. Because of the covenants, Israelites believed God had decided to throw his lot in with that of Israel's. God had decided Israel's fate would have consequences for God's own fate. God had decided Israel's enemies were God's enemies. God's partiality towards Israel was God's decision and this partiality and intimacy were at the heart of the God-Israel relationship. Jewish laments and Wiesel's laments make no sense apart from this understanding of the intertwined fates of God and Israel.

5) *The Reputation of God*

The community lament tradition shows a great deal of concern for the reputation of God. And this concern stems from the assumption that Israel's fate and the fate of God are inseparable. The psalmist fears for the honor of God, for the sake of God's name he begs for deliverance. Such concern for God's reputation and honor stems also from the intimate relation between God and Israel. When the psalmist mentions the insults of the enemies it reflects the deep concern Israel has for her covenant partner, God.

Three times in Psalm 74 the psalmist cautions God to be aware of the attack of the enemy on God's name, "Is the enemy to revile your name forever?" And in v. 18 God is warned, "Remember this

O Lord, how the enemy scoffs, and an impious people reviles your name." Or, as in v. 22, "remember how the impious scoff at you all day." In Psalm 79:6 God is encouraged, "pour out your anger on the kingdoms that do not call on your name"; in 79:10, the psalmist asks God, "Why should the nations say, 'Where is their God?'"

In a similar vein, Psalm 83 calls upon God to act and save God's reputation. In Psalm 83:5–6 we can see Israel's belief that the name of Israel and the name of God are intertwined. In v. 5 the psalmist reports to God the words of the enemy, "They say, 'Come let us wipe them out as a nation; let the name of Israel be remembered no more!' Yes, they conspire with one accord; against you they make a covenant." The psalm concludes with an appeal to God to act for the sake of God's reputation. "Fill their faces with shame that they may seek your name, O Lord, let them know that you alone, whose name is the Lord, are the most high over all the earth."

It must be stressed that Israel's constant concern and attention to God's reputation is evidence of her relationship with God whereby each partner is concerned for the welfare of the other. Israel looks out for God's reputation because they are married to one another. Any attack on God is an attack on Israel as well. And any attack on Israel is an attack on God.

6) *God Is Affected by Prayer*

To understand why the ancient Hebrews and Elie Wiesel thought God could and would be affected, influenced, and moved by prayer, it is important to recognize that God had a reputation of being willing to change, to evolve the divine mind or plans. It was not merely that God was willing, by God's grace, to act on Israel's behalf. It was the persuasiveness of the argument or prayer that would and could convince God to act. Though some scholars express doubts that God can be compelled to act apart from God's grace or liberty, the community lament psalms depict a God who can be motivated, reminded, accused, commanded, questioned, and even chastised. It was not a matter of God's grace or condescension. The issue was whether the content of the prayer convinced God to act.

CHAPTER TWO: ISRAEL LAMENTS ITS RELATIONSHIP TO GOD

Remember: the point of the lament prayers is to convince God to act. These prayers abound with imperative petitions offering God concrete reasons as to why God should act on Israel's behalf as well as commanding God to do so immediately. Now! The traditional religious portrait of a sovereign omnipotent God who knows, plans, and has everything under control would certainly have problems with a description of a God who has a bad memory or who on occasion falls asleep. However, when you read the lament prayers you recognize that the Israelites believed God was vulnerable to forgetting his relationship to Israel or of being asleep when Israel needed him most. Such an understanding does not seem to reflect badly on the character of God. Rather it reflects Israel's experience of a problematic deity. For Israel, God was one who could forget and who could fall asleep. So, God was also one who should be reminded, convinced, and awakened. All this was cemented by those two fundamental convictions discussed earlier: God's love of Israel and God's commitment to justice.

In Psalm 44 the issue of God's forgetfulness is raised. The psalmist contrasts Israel's remembrance of God with God's forgetfulness of his people. In v. 18, he writes, "All this has come upon us, though we have not forgotten you." Then in v. 21, "Why do you forget our affliction and oppression?" Psalm 74:2 also contains imperatives calling on God to "remember your congregation . . . Remember Mount Zion."

There are many imperatives intent upon awakening God. Besides being commanded to remember, God is petitioned to "rouse yourself . . . awake" (Ps 44:24), "rise up!" (Ps 44:27) "Pay attention" (74:20), "Arise" (Ps 74:22), "Pour out your anger" (Ps 79:6), "Stir yourself up" (Ps 80:3), "turn again, O God of hosts! Look down from heaven and see; regard this vine" (Ps 80:15). The psalmist does not appear to be shy in confronting God. He prays to God in intimacy, as one lover would address another; he asks questions, motivates, demands, cajoles, and calls God to be faithful to God's beloved. This is not naïve utilitarian manipulation of the deity! Indeed, Israel is convinced that her God can be affected and moved by the words of the prayer. Remember,

God's relationship to Israel is fundamental to God's very existence and Israel's relationship with God is fundamental to her very existence. Anything that threatens either one of these two partners is understood as a fundamental threat to the other. It is in the context of such intimacy that God is understood as being affected by the prayers of his people.

7) *Sin in the Community Lament Psalms*

The lament prayers in the Jewish Bible are concerned with the anger of God. It was assumed by some that God's anger and punishment were caused by Israel's sin. That would make sense but is not acceptable to the psalmist. Just listen to the words of the community lament psalms concerning the anger of God: Psalm 44:10 charges God, "You have cast us off and abased us." Psalm 60:3 declares, "O God, you have been angry." Psalm 74:1 questions, "Why does your anger smoke against the sheep of your pasture?" Psalm 79:5 cries, "How long, O God? Will you be angry forever? Will your jealous wrath burn like fire?" Psalm 80:5 asks, "O Lord God of Hosts, how long will you be angry with your people's prayers?" Psalm 83:2 demands, "O God. Do not keep silence, do not hold your peace or be still O God." And Psalm 89:47 echoes, "How long O Lord? Will you hide yourself forever? How long will your wrath burn like fire?"

Is the anger of God the result of Israel's sin? And if so, is that sufficient reason for God to abandon Israel to her enemies when God has previously promised in an assortment of covenants that he would not? The writers of these psalms are willing to grant that Israel has sinned against God but argues this is no reason God should be endlessly angry or remain silent. Psalm 79:8–9 speaks of the sins of the fathers as well as the transgressions of the Israel of his time: "Do not remember against us the iniquities of our forefathers; let your compassion come speedily to meet us, for we are brought very low. Help us, O God of our salvation, for the glory of your name; deliver us, and forgive our sins, for your name's sake." Other than this text, there is no other mention of Israel's sin in the community

CHAPTER TWO: ISRAEL LAMENTS ITS RELATIONSHIP TO GOD

lament psalms. There is no mention of repentance or confession of sin. Israel does not appear to be struggling with a collective guilty conscience. Why not? Because the silence of God is not necessarily associated with the sinfulness of Israel.

There is a difference between the way traditional Jews and many Christians understand the word *sin*. For Jews, sin is an action which misses the mark, like an arrow missing a target. For many Western Christians, sin is a condition in which a person knows what is right yet does what is wrong. This is referred to as "original sin" since it is believed by some Christians that all human beings have inherited this condition from their very origins. Jews believe human beings are born neutral with a freedom to act well or not. Some Christians believe human beings are born unfree, captive to the power of sin until they are freed by the power of Christ. Jews believe humans have the capacity to act well. Some Christians believe the power of sin has incapacitated people from acting well. (See more about this in chapter 4.)

Just listen to Psalm 44:18-22: "All this has come upon us, though we have not forgotten you, or been false to your covenant. Our heart has not turned back, nor have our steps departed from your way." It is not that the psalmist sees himself or the people of Israel as being sinless. It is just that he is convinced that whatever sin the people had committed it does not excuse God's silence or indifference.

Whether or not Israel had sinned against God did not matter. The prayer appeals to the God-Israel relationship over and above any reference to sin. This is not to say that the anger of God was not caused by Israel's sin. It is to say that sins of Israel are not the main point. The point seems to be, whether Israel has sinned or has not sinned, God is obligated to act on behalf of the God-Israel relationship. There are some things more important than sin and God needs to hear it, adhere to it, and act justly.

One of the best examples of this is Psalm 79. In this psalm the prayer admits that Israel has sinned but v. 5 questions God concerning the duration and appropriateness of his anger. In v. 6 the psalmist implies that if God really wants to act justly, he will pour out his anger, not on Israel, but on the nations, who are causing pain to Israel and God. Sin is important but it is not that important! Verses 8–9 continue to emphasize this theme. The psalmist confesses the sins of the fathers and the people. This does not deny the present importance of Israel's sin but instead says there are terrible things happening that are more important than any sin committed by the people. But how do we know this is so? Because if you look at v. 9 you will see appeals being made for God to act for the sake of his name and v. 10 brings up the reputation of God as well as the pain of Israel. And this is followed in vv. 11–12 with an emphasis on the plight of the prisoners as well as a description of the taunts of the enemy directed at God. What has happened to the issue of sin raised in vv. 8–9? Its importance is obviously secondary to the evil Israel is experiencing. The existence of Israel is being threatened and nothing is more important, not even sin! I would even go so far as to assert that in all the corporate prayers for help in the Jewish Bible, the appeal to justice and the intimate relationship between God and Israel takes precedence over the issue of sin. When the existence of Israel as a nation was threatened, she immediately appealed to God to think of their intimate relationship over and above any transgression of the nation.

There have been some rabbis who have proposed that the Holocaust is in some way retribution for the sins of Jewish assimilation to modernity. When we look at the evidence of the lament psalms as well as Wiesel's writings, we can see that such views are misguided. Having studied and taught the Holocaust for many years, I am convinced the Holocaust was an act of pure evil and had nothing to do with God. Attempts to exonerate God by blaming Israel's sin *will not work and are an insult to any kind of honest faith.*

8) Israel Expects God to Act in History

This theme at first seems obvious. Of course, Israelites expected God to act. Why else would they be praying to God? Some contemporary Jewish scholars, such as Rabbi Harold Kushner, have asserted that after the Holocaust, we need to realize God is not

CHAPTER TWO: ISRAEL LAMENTS ITS RELATIONSHIP TO GOD

all powerful.[2] Perhaps God is only able to give human beings strength and courage to make it through the present catastrophe. In fact, Kushner asserts, *why* is the wrong question because it concentrates on the past. Instead, we should ask *when* these things happen how we can survive.

Praying for God to act historically is seen by Kushner as naïve and mistaken. Those Jews standing in the Nazi gas chambers crying to God to save them were praying for the impossible. While Wiesel asserts that God *failed* to act, Kushner, on the other hand, asserts it was not that God was unwilling to act. According to Kushner, God was *unable* to act. After the Holocaust must we admit the laments were wrong, and Kushner is right? Was God simply unable to act? And if we go along with the biblical lament prayers, how can we explain the silence of God in our own time?

In the community lament prayers God is directed to act in a concrete and visible manner. We need to appreciate the historical hope and expectations these ancients possessed. Wiesel's expectations and questions regarding God make no sense unless we understand why the people who prayed back then did so too. Their expectation was God would and could act in history on their behalf. The fact that God did not act did not stop the lament prayers.

The Israelites in Psalm 44 assert in verse 11, "You have made us like sheep for the slaughter and have scattered us among the nations." Listen to this cacophony of imperatives calling on God to act and act now. Psalm 44:27 reads, "Rise up and come to our help! Deliver us for the sake of your steadfast love." Psalm 60:3 prays, "O' grant us help against the foe, for vain is the help of man!" Psalm 74:22 calls, "Arise, O God, plead your cause." Psalm 79:6 exhorts, "Pour out your anger on the nations." Psalm 79:12 echoes, "Return sevenfold into the bosom of our neighbors." Psalm 80:3 sounds similarly, "Stir up your might, and come to save us!" Psalm 83:10 recalls, "Do to them as you did to Midian." Psalm 83:16 cries, " Pursue them with your tempest and terrify them with your hurricane!" In these verses God is commanded to act like God. For the sake of the God-Israel relationship God

2. See Kushner, "When Bad Things Happen to Good People."

is implored to pour out his wrath on the nations. He is called upon to act concretely because his people are being oppressed and afflicted. Inherent in these prayers is an understanding of God willing and able to act in history.

What can we gather from this investigation? Israel understood its existence as an act of creation by God in history. God was seen as one able and willing to act in history. God was not limited even by human freedom. The intimacy between God and Israel allowed and compelled the Israelites to hope God would yet act to save his people. When God did not act, the only thing to be done was to raise questions and accusations as an extension of their faith that God would still act like God.

As I examined and reexamined the theological rationale for the laments, it began to make sense to me how Wiesel could raise his questions. I have since concluded these laments and Wiesel are right. If you are going to believe in a God who created the universe, you must conclude God has extraordinary ability and power to act in human history. When God appears not to do so, all we can do is raise our questions and complaints as honestly as possible.

It also became clear to me if I was going to continue to be an intelligent religious person, whose relatives had been murdered in the Nazi camps, I needed to adopt a lament perspective in my own life. I wanted to continue to believe in the God of Israel, but I could not resolve the silence of God during the Holocaust.

Chapter Three: *God Laments His Relationship with Israel*

The idea that Israel could be disappointed by God was a shocking revelation to me. The converse, God being disappointed in Israel, was not. Every bad thing that happens to Israel is blamed on God's displeasure. Over and over the books of the prophets outline how Israel has failed to live up to God's expectations. God can also lament and complain about Israel's behavior. But as Israel tenaciously refuses to give up on God, God, with an equal tenacity, does not give up on Israel. The tenacity of God is part and parcel of the intimacy and irrevocability of the covenants. This is most evident when we turn to the biblical prophets.

Contrary to much popular belief, the prophets in the Jewish Bible did not predict the future. Instead, the prophets were people who spoke the truth about God. They spoke concretely and exactly about the sins of Israel, and they called people back to morality and obedience to God's commandments. Their central purpose was to persuade people to repent. But there was more going on. The prophetic writings, in addition to calls to repent, remind us over and over about the intimate relationship between God and his people. God is pictured as being angry at the people's sin, but that does not do away with God's love for Israel.

In the same way the Psalms emphasize God as the creator of Israel, the prophets emphasize that very same theme. Consider Isaiah 43:1–4 and 44:1–2, "But now thus says the Lord, he who created you, O Jacob, he who formed you O' Israel: Fear not, for I have redeemed you; I have called you by name, you are mine." And 43:4: "Because you are precious in my eyes, and honored, and I love you, I give men in return for you, peoples in exchange for your life." So even though sin, wrath, and punishment have taken place, the God-Israel relationship remains intact. There has been forgiveness of past sins (43:25), but the motivation for this forgiveness was not merely the grace of an impersonal God. Rather it was the intimacy and depth of the God-Israel covenant marriage relationship that appears to have moved God to act. The creator of Israel is in love with and committed to this people.

Isaiah 44:1–2 reads, "But now, hear O' Jacob my servant, Israel whom I have chosen! Thus says the Lord who made you, who formed you from the womb and will help you: fear not, O Jacob my servant, Jeshu'run whom I have chosen." The promise of God to act on Israel's behalf is motivated by God's special relationship to this particular people. They are God's chosen, his servants; he created them. For all the importance given to forgiveness of sins in Isaiah, it appears that sin is a secondary theme compared to the significance of the God-Israel relationship.

Remember, one of the central themes in the lament psalms is the forgetfulness of God. Again and again God is being told to remember and not to forget what is happening to "your people." In Isaiah 49 the prophet asserts that God is unable to forget. Verses 14–16 in Isaiah 49 read, "But Zion said, 'the Lord has forsaken me, my Lord has forgotten me.' Can a woman forget her sucking child, that she should have no compassion for the son of her womb? Even they may forget, yet I will not forget you. Behold, I have engraved you on the palms of my hands, your walls are continually before me." Through these words we hear something beyond merely a deity graciously forgiving the sins of his people. Here, rather, is a deep love relationship that exists beyond any demands for justice. This description of this profound relationship between God and

CHAPTER THREE: GOD LAMENTS HIS RELATIONSHIP WITH ISRAEL

Israel indicates that though the transgressions of Israel were taken seriously by God and even punished with severity, they were never sufficient to break the intimate bond of the two.

It is also important to remember that Elie Wiesel's and my own questions and accusations of God are rooted in the intimacy of God's relationship to the Jewish people. Isaiah 54:5-8 describes God as the husband who deserted his wife because of her transgressions. Nonetheless, the husband returns to his wife because of his continuing love for her. As vv. 5-8 reads,

> For your maker is your husband, the Lord of hosts is his name; and the holy one of Israel is your redeemer, the God of the whole earth he is called. For the Lord has called you like a wife forsaken and grieved in spirit, like a wife of youth when she is cast off, says your God. For a brief moment I forsook you, but with great compassion I will gather you. In overflowing wrath for a moment, I hid my face from you, but with everlasting love I will have compassion on you, says the Lord, your redeemer.

In this metaphorical analogy, the poet Isaiah describes a husband who, having deserted his wife, decides to return, proclaims his love for the wife, and in v. 10 promises never to leave her again: "For the mountains may depart and the hills be removed, but my steadfast love shall not depart from you, and my covenant of peace shall not be removed, says the Lord who has compassion on you." Despite God's overwhelming disappointment in Israel, this text makes it clear that the forgiveness given to Israel by God, as described in Second Isaiah, was not a part of some forensic juridical process. Rather, this forgiveness stems from the relationship of love that existed between Israel and her God. The love of God for Israel was understood as being prior to and over and above any sin committed by the people, over and above God's disappointment. Of course, Israel was aware of and confessed its sins. The oracles of God's wrath and punishment in Isaiah bear witness to this awareness on her part. However, it should also be clear any sin committed by the people was not seen as sufficient reason for God to break God's relationship with his people. Israel believed nothing could separate her from the love of God. Covenants could be broken, renewed, or made again; wrath and punishment could be deserved and occur, but the God-Israel relationship was understood to be an irrevocable constant.

In so many texts, particularly in the prophets, we see the mingling of justice and love. Whatever justice God was engaged in, it was always tempered by God's love and compassion of Israel. We see this graphically in the book of Hosea. Hosea begins with God's command for the prophet to enter a relationship with a harlot, as well as have children with her. The three children the couple will have are to be called, respectively, Jezreel (God sows), connoting the punishment to be done to Israel; Lo-ruhamah (Not Pitied), referring to the lack of pity for Israel; and Lo-ammi (Not My People), explained by Hosea 1:8 as follows, "Call his name Lo-ammi (Not My People) for you are not my people and I am not yours." Having detailed the significance of each of the children's names, the prophet goes on to express the wrath and punishment of God. Justice will be done to Israel. Sin has its consequences.

But suddenly, in Hosea 2:16, the mood changes. God is quoted as saying, "Therefore, behold, I will allure her, and bring her into the wilderness and speak tenderly to her." Despite all of Israel's failures, God is pictured as being tenaciously optimistic and determined concerning the reconciliation between himself and Israel. Using the intimate language of the husband/wife relation, the prophet writes, "And in that day, says the Lord, you will call me 'my husband' and no longer will you call me my Baal." Verses 21–22 speak of the betrothal of God to his bride, Israel. "And I will betroth you to me forever; I will betroth you to me in righteousness and in justice, in steadfast love, and in mercy. I will betroth you to me in faithfulness and you shall know the Lord." Finally, v. 25b declares, "And I will say to Lo-ammi (Not My People), you are my People; and he shall say, you are my God."

In Hosea 3:1, God is pictured as telling the prophet to return to his harlot wife despite her transgressions. "And the Lord said to me, go again, love a woman beloved of a paramour and [who] is an adulteress; even as the Lord loves the people of Israel,

CHAPTER THREE: GOD LAMENTS HIS RELATIONSHIP WITH ISRAEL

though they turn to other gods and love cakes of raisins." Hosea's metaphorical picture of the pain and anguish God undergoes as the spurned lover is instructive for us in trying to understand the God-Israel relationship. The faithful God is pictured as being married to the faithless Israel. In Hosea 6:4 God is described as asking, "What shall I do with you, O Judah? Your love is like a morning cloud, like the dew that goes away early." This faithlessness on the part of Israel brings God's justice, anger, and punishment. But, and this is key, the wrath of God cannot and does not separate the deity from his people.

In later chapters of Hosea, God is portrayed as one committed to Israel: "How can I give you up, Ephraim, how can I hand you over O' Israel! . . . My heart recoils within me, my compassion grows warm and tender. I will not execute my fierce anger. I will not again destroy Ephraim; for I am God and not man, the holy one in your midst, and I will not come to destroy."

Yet, in the book of Hosea, the sin of Israel is taken seriously. As a matter of justice, Israel will be punished. However, as far as Hosea is concerned, neither the commission of sin nor the wrath and punishment of the deity can destroy the intimate relationship between God and Israel. Indeed, in 14:5 the prophet has God say, "I will heal their faithlessness; I will love them freely, for my anger has turned from them." For the Jewish people, the justice and love of God are inextricably linked. Hence, when Elie Wiesel appeals to the justice of God he is implicitly appealing to the love of God for Israel and the reciprocal love of Israel for God. For Wiesel the issue is fidelity on God's part.

Justice and love are again intermingled in the book of Jeremiah. Jeremiah believes Israel has sinned and has no grounds of appeal to God. In 14:10 God dismisses their lament appeals: "They have loved to wander thus, they have not restrained their feet; therefore, the Lord does not accept them, now he will remember their iniquity and punish their sins." In vv. 19–21 another lament is made on behalf of the people. Appeals are made to God's name (v. 21), the throne of God, as well as the covenant (v. 21). Once again God is adamant about his anger towards Israel. As 15:1 reads: "then the

Lord said to me, though Moses and Samuel stood before me, yet my heart would not turn toward this people." The judgment oracles of Jeremiah reveal that the relationship between God and his people does not spare them from suffering the consequences of their sins. Israel has been faithless to her God. The community has not lived up to God's expectations. God is disappointed. It would appear Israel has no grounds with which to appeal her situation.

And yet, in Jeremiah the well-deserved punishment for sin is not the last word. Since God is inextricably linked or married to Israel, there will be a new covenant with which to strengthen their marriage. This new covenant written about in chapter 31 is made so that the God-Israel relationship would no longer have to suffer the pain of exile. And God talks about that relationship in 31:1–3: "At that time, says the Lord, I will be the God of all the families of that time, says the Lord, I will be the God of all the families of Israel, and they shall be my people. Thus, says the Lord, the people who survived the sword found grace in the wilderness; when Israel sought for rest, the Lord appeared to him from afar. I have loved you with an everlasting love. Therefore, I have continued my faithfulness to you."

Here we see how God is bound to a particular people. To break this relationship with Israel was constitutionally impossible. Their pain was God's pain. Their punishment for sins committed created pain for God; their faithfulness and love were God's hope. The new covenant made with Israel in Jeremiah was based on and made for the God-Israel relationship.

When you read Wiesel's books, you do not see him asking God for forgiveness. Nor does Wiesel ask God to ignore the sins of the Jewish people. Wiesel wants God to act because God is God and God's name is tied to the people Israel. God has covenantal responsibilities, obligations, and commitments to the Jewish people. And God's name is tied to those covenants. God has cast his lot with the Jewish people and so is compelled to act for the sake of his name. How did the Jewish people come to believe all of that? The prophet Ezekiel talks about why God will act on behalf of the Israelites despite their sins. The sins of Israel are not unimportant.

CHAPTER THREE: GOD LAMENTS HIS RELATIONSHIP WITH ISRAEL

They are not just ultimately so. God's fate is tied to Israel's fate, causing God to act despite their sin. In Ezekiel 36:22–32 we read, "And I will vindicate the holiness of my great name, which has been profaned among the nations, and which you have profaned among them; and the nations will know that I am the Lord, says the Lord God, when through you I vindicate my holiness before their eyes." Isn't this precisely what the prayers of the community lament psalms were asking God to do?

The relationship between God and Israel is certainly strained in Ezekiel. Yes, Israel seems to have believed God would not abandon his people. It would be easy to be critical of such a belief and to emphasize God's universal concern for the entire creation. This particularistic Jewish belief can sound arrogant or exclusive, but that is not its intention. God established a relationship with Israel and God's name is at risk of being shamed and insulted. God being tied to the Jewish people is God's decision. This decision binds God to involvement in the vicissitudes of Israel's history. But this being bound to a particular people is not understood as taking away from God's freedom to act. It was God's free act to bind his justice and his love to Israel. In Ezekiel 36:32, the text seems to be clear that God is acting for "the sake of my holy name." It does not say God is acting for the sake of his love for Israel. However, certain elements of the chapter lead us to a different conclusion. In v. 32 we hear God being critical of Israel, "Be ashamed and confounded for your ways, O house of Israel." This scolding is reminiscent of much of Ezekiel, in which God chastises Israel for the way she has behaved. No one can doubt the prophet believed God was appropriately angry at his people. So, when God acts despite their sin to save Israel, can we not conclude God is acting because he loves Israel despite her sins?

There is a fascinating text in Ezekiel where the prophet writes about how God first met Israel and their early romance. Look at Ezekiel 16, the allegory of the unfaithful wife. In this text Israel is pictured as the female whom God finds deserted and alone in an open field. God is moved by her situation and decides to take care of her. God marries Israel and enters into a covenant with her. As v. 8 reads, "When I passed by you again and looked upon you, behold you were at the age for love; and I spread my skirt over you, and covered your nakedness; yea, I plighted by troth to you and entered into a covenant with you, says the Lord your God, and you became mine." The reference in this text to first the plighting of troth and then secondarily the making of a covenant is significant. The two acts are not simultaneous; they are sequential. The point is that covenants may come and go, may be obeyed or disobeyed, may require renewal and repentance, but God's relationship to his people remains constant. The relationship between God and Israel is not built and based on only covenant agreement but on intimate love.

This emphasis on the separation of their intimate relation and the covenant is made clear in Ezekiel 16:59–63. For over fifty-eight verses in chapter 16 the prophet describes how Israel has continuously broken the covenant with God. No one can doubt the anger, pain, and disappointment of God in these verses. Israel has broken the covenant. It no longer exists. On what basis then can God act to save his people? Certainly not on the basis of any covenant, since Israel has been unfaithful and broken all the covenants. Yet, in v. 59 God declares that he will make a new covenant with Israel. Verse 60 reads: "Yet I will remember my covenant with you in the days of your youth, and I will establish with you an everlasting covenant." This is quite something! God is angry and punishes Israel. But God remembers the way they met and his intimate love for Israel. Accordingly, God acts to deliver Israel, not because Israel is so beautiful or faithful. Rather, God acts through God's forgiveness and new covenant making to strengthen the God-Israel relationship.

Everything we have just examined in Ezekiel is happening in the context of what historians will call the Babylonian exile. The temple has been destroyed, the king is dead, the old covenants are gone, and the people have been taken into exile. It appears God has abandoned them. The Babylonian exile created a major crisis for continued Jewish belief or trust in God.

CHAPTER THREE: GOD LAMENTS HIS RELATIONSHIP WITH ISRAEL

The covenants—believed to be unbreakable bonds—between God and the people have been shattered. God's dwelling place has been desecrated. God is forced to leave the temple.

It is then fair to say the exile, in that way, can be seen as akin to the Holocaust in that God's faithfulness to the Jewish people had been called into question. One of the books in the Bible which grapples with the justice of God is the book of Job. As a part of what has come to be called wisdom literature, no book is more controversial than Job.

Chapter Four: *The Book of Job and the Holocaust*

Biblical wisdom literature is everything that isn't a book of Torah or Law (Genesis, Exodus, Leviticus, Numbers and Deuteronomy) or the writing of a prophet (Isaiah, Jeremiah, Amos, etc.)

Wisdom literature includes Ruth, Proverbs, Songs of Solomon, Psalms, and the grandaddy of them all, Job. No book of the Bible has been as puzzling as this book. The book of Job calls into question the belief that everything that happens occurs because it is God's will. In the book of Job, Job's ten children are murdered because God is making a wager with Satan. This is not the Satan of the New Testament. This Satan is a messenger of God sent to roam the earth and report back to God. This Satan reports that Job is faithful, but only because something bad has not happened to him. So, God wagers with Satan that even if something terrible were to happen to Job, he, Job, would remain faithful.

At first, Job accepts his fate, but as the book progresses, Job rebels. While his friends chastise him and say that what has happened to him is a result of his sin and that he must have deserved the retribution of having his ten children be killed, Job says no! Instead, Job questions and accuses God of injustice. He argues with his friends, his so-called comforters. Finally, after all these

CHAPTER FOUR: THE BOOK OF JOB AND THE HOLOCAUST

words, God shows up to answer Job. But his answer is no answer. He asks Job where Job was when God created the world. God says Job was right and his friends were wrong. God indicates that while Job's lament was right, it was not wise. And Job submits to God and repents of his words.

After the Holocaust, it is precisely this submission to God Elie Wiesel disputes. Wiesel says Job should never have let God off the hook.[1] I think he's right. So with Wiesel's criticism of Job in mind, I wrote a midrash about the book of Job and the Holocaust. In it, Job becomes everyman. Job suffers. Job laments. Job *accuses* God. Job *demands* an explanation.

The Hebrew word *midrash* refers to an interpretation of a specific biblical text—in this case Job. A midrash makes explicit what is implicit in a text. It fills in the white spaces around the letters and the words and the gaps in the story itself. A midrash is not fanciful. Nor is it created out of thin air. A midrash enquires how a particular text would speak to a contemporary situation and develops a newly relevant truth out of that text.

I wrote this midrash after hearing Elie Wiesel's lament that even though Job challenged and questioned God, even after he lamented and accused God, Job did not go far enough to insist that God explain the existence of undeserved suffering in the world, particularly as it related to the Holocaust. Wiesel maintained that just as there was no justice for Job, there was no justice for the six million Jews who were murdered in the Holocaust. And so, just as Job wanted an explanation, Wiesel—and I—wanted an explanation. This midrash was an attempt to provide an explanation, to answer Job's questions, Wiesel's questions, and my questions.[2]

Job after Auschwitz

Eighty-five years ago, in the small Polish village of Krasnobrod, the prophet Job came to live with the Jews of Poland. Among the

1. Wiesel, Augustana Lecture.
2. A version of this midrash was originally published in *Interpretation*, July 1999.

twenty-eight hundred Jews of the village, Job encountered refugees from other small towns and hamlets across Poland who told tales of what had happened in their shtetels. The Nazis had come, rounded up all the Jews, and marched them out of town. The men, women, girls, and boys were made to undress. They were forced to dig holes in the ground. Then they were shot and thrown into the open graves. Job, who had, in days gone by, believed when told that his own children had been murdered, now refused to believe what his eyes had just seen. He said, "It cannot be. It cannot be that God could see what is happening here and would not be moved to stop the killing. It cannot be God would allow so many innocent people, so many children to be slaughtered. After all they are God's people. God loves them. It cannot be God could be so indifferent."

Job had been in Krasnobrod for almost a month, observing how these poor people struggled to live from day to day. They suffered from hunger and poverty. Yet, they tenaciously held on to their faith in God. Job learned that Jews had lived in the town for over seven hundred years. There were four rabbis in that town. There were teachers, scholars, mechanics, merchants, doctors, peddlers, beggars, mothers, fathers, grandmothers, grandfathers, and many children. One Jewish family, the Lichtenfelds, caught Job's attention. They lived in a tiny hut, a husband, a wife, and four daughters. In many ways they reminded Job of his own family.

The day the Lichtenfelds were murdered was a day like any other day. It was spring and the sky was a brilliant blue. The trees were beginning to bud. The birds made their sweet noises without noticing what was happening. It was indeed a beautiful day. Job, a non-Jew, followed the march of the Jews out of town. In stunned silence he watched as they were all ordered to undress. In silence he stared as they were made to dig their graves. In silence, he watched as the Lichtenfelds were all shot. Job watched as they each dropped into the holes in the ground. As he walked away in shock, Job began to see where he had been wrong, so long ago, in the land of Uz, his home. He remembered the death of his ten children. He remembered when it had come time for him to stand face-to-face with the Almighty,

CHAPTER FOUR: THE BOOK OF JOB AND THE HOLOCAUST

how he had backed down before God. Job realized he had submitted to God, not out of wisdom or renewed faith, but out of fear.

Job walked back to Krasnobrod filled with shame and guilt for not having done something to prevent the massacre. He saw the town had been burned to the ground. The only building left standing was the small synagogue. And as he approached the smoldering ruins, Job saw the Torah scrolls lying on the ground unraveled and still burning. He bent down and rescued a piece of the parchment. He stared at its Hebrew characters and recognized the words as a portion of the story of the sacrifice of Isaac. In that story God had acted to stop the killing. Job sat down on the ground and wept.

This time there were no friends to comfort or to accuse Job. The Jews of Krasnobrod had disappeared from the face of the earth. And Job, sitting alone in the decimated village, decided he would once again approach God. This time, he resolved to ask better questions. This time he would do a better job of confronting God. This time he would not let God off the hook. Job raised his voice and began to speak:

"O God, I rise from my submission to speak once more to you. This day, I speak with plain language; I approach you and demand your response to my plea. I approach you as one who has traveled to and fro on the earth. I have seen the killing of your children. The babies have been murdered before your very eyes. But you have remained silent. We have heard you are a God who sees everything. But what does it mean for your eyes to see the children you love butchered? Why do you remain silent? Do you remain silent because you are committed to the free will of your creatures? So have said comforters in your defense throughout history. Do you remain indifferent because you are eager for humans to take responsibility for their own lives? So say others. Do you not care because you are busy testing the faith of your committed ones? So say the pious comforters. Do you turn away from watching because the slaughter of your children is part of some mysterious plan, which we are unable to decipher? So say the comforters eager to protect you. Do you not hear the cries of your children because you are thinking, one day I will send the messiah to destroy evil and save them? So say the comforters who are too frightened to tell you it is too late. Do you remain mute while your children are buried alive because you think it is enough that you cry with the victims? Some comforters assure us that you are suffering with the ones being killed. They are too frightened to tell you the truth.

"O' God, are you offended at my impertinence and arrogance? Or do you even care that I am hurling these questions at your face? Are you willing to meet me in the breach?

"Today, there are all kinds of comforters making excuses over your silence, but I will not accept their theological gymnastics. I will speak freely. May you take offense at my words that they might move you action! O God of Abraham and Sarah, Isaac and Rebecca, Jacob and Rachel, be shocked and come to Kransnobrod. God of Moses, Joshua, Hanna, and Samuel, arise and go to Treblinka. God of the Jewish people, awake and go to Auschwitz, see what is being done. O God, do not slumber; go to Buchenwald, to Theresienstadt, to Warsaw, to Lublin, to Zamoscz, to Belzec. Clear your eyes and see how your servants, the Lichtenfelds, have been murdered. Did you see how they stood naked before their graves? There they were: Josef, Zeiftel, and their daughters. Did you see how Zeiftel held the little ones close to her? O God, open your eyes and look as no one but you can look. See what madness has happened to your people, your creation, the people of Israel. God of deliverance and liberation, can you explain your silence in the face of such atrocity? Oh, but God, if you could render explainable what is inexplicable, then would you not be committing an act of blasphemy against your own name?

"I wake up in the middle of the night and I wonder if it is possible for you, O God, to be frightened? Are you disturbed by Sobibor and Sachsenhausen? Do you, the Lord of the universe, quiver with fear at the doors of Mathausen and Bergen Belsen? God of all creation, do you stand at the gates of Birkenau and tremble at what man can do to man? Can the creator be frightened at what the creatures have done? Can a God stand in awe and silence before such stark madness and still claim to be God? It says in the Jewish Scriptures that the blood of Abel cried to you from the ground. If the blood of one man can cause such an outcry that you stop and notice, what does the cry and blood of a million and a half children do to the divine mind?

CHAPTER FOUR: THE BOOK OF JOB AND THE HOLOCAUST

Does it frighten you that so many children were killed? How can you watch and listen without being moved by their blood?
   "Arise and meet me once again. Speak with me face-to-face that I may come to know what keeps you unmoved before the cries and screams of all your people. You are God and I am not. And yet I come before you to speak the truth. You have said you have the power to harness and defeat evil. Having created human beings in your image, with the capacity for evil, do you now merely shake your head wishing it had turned out better? O my God, you know about the number of children, do you not? In those days long ago, we are told, you caused the flood that drowned so many; you smote the first born of the Egyptians, and unforgivably you brought about the death of my ten children. How is it you can watch the death of so many children and not be moved to act to prevent such killing again?

   "You who were so moved by the blood of Abel, you who could not bear to watch the shedding of Isaac's blood, you who passed over the bloodstained doors of your people, how can you not be moved by the shed blood of a million and a half children? Does their blood not cry to you from the ground? Is their cry not loud enough to reach your ears? Do you weep for your children like a sad, weak, old man, compassionate but unable to act for lack of strength? O, that you would rise up and speak to your servant who calls upon you to explain yourself in the presence of so many dead.

   "Do you remember who you are? Are the words in our Scriptures truth or lies? Are the promises you spoke your words or ours? Do you remember what you said, what you promised, what you did, what you urged us to believe? What do you remember, O God? Have you become senile? I remember my children, the beauty of their eyes, the innocence of their laughter, the naivete of their faith, and the injustice of their deaths. Can a father forget his children? Can I forget the wailing of my wife as she was forced to look upon the corpses of her children? I want to forget, but I cannot forget. No night goes by without my mourning their deaths. But are you a God who remembers? What does it mean to remember the deaths of so many children? O' God, how do you bear the memory of the small ones who screamed with an unquenchable scream?

"The wise man says, 'In memory lies redemption.' Is it not time for you to redeem yourself? What would or could such a redemption look like? Is it too late? Answer your servant Job and I will respond. Ask for their forgiveness, and I will approach the dead on your behalf. Speak and be heard by a just man. Speak, if you have the courage to speak. I stand here in the breach and call upon you, O God, to repent of your silence."

Suddenly, from the burning ashes of the synagogue, God answered Job: "You still do not know that I am God, and you are not. Your speech is just but not wise. The blood of the children has given you the passion to speak but not the wisdom to understand. Would you accuse me of wrongdoing? Would you accuse me of not acting like God? You have asked without shame and I am compelled to answer your words. I do not evade your eyes. I look at you face-to-face. I have seen and I remember! I have seen all there is to see, and there are no acts of human atrocity I have not seen. From Krasnobrod to Auschwitz, I have seen, I know, and I remember. I have heard their cries and I know their pain and suffering. I have not been deaf to their wailing.

"You ask me why I have been silent. Have I been silent? I ask why you have been indifferent. I have given you my Torah which teaches you how to stay sane and avoid chaos. And yet the killing goes on from generation to generation. You bemoan the death of the children, yet you are the ones who have continued to kill. From Krasnobrod to Auschwitz to Belzec, you, not I, have shed the blood of children, my children. Know this: salvation never comes through death. When your Scriptures picture me as a killer of children and a shedder of blood, they do not speak the truth. From the children of the flood to the children of Egypt, from Abel to Isaac to Jeremiah, to your own children, death was never my will.

"Job, gird yourself like a man and explain to me why human beings have not listened to my teaching? Have I indeed been silent? Have I not tried to teach you to adhere to my commandments that you might be truly humane? Where have I failed to instruct you, cajole you, transform you, convert you, urge you, even intimidate you into action for one another? If I have been silent it is to encourage you to

CHAPTER FOUR: THE BOOK OF JOB AND THE HOLOCAUST

look at what you have done. You charge me with not preventing evil. It is you who violate all moral limits and boundaries I have set for you. And you have the nerve to charge me with wrongdoing?"

When God was finished speaking, this time Job did not just bow down and submit. "What you have said, O God, is beside the point. To speak in generalities about the human condition is to ignore specifically what happened to the Lichtenfelds. A mother and a father and their daughters were murdered. They were good, faithful, innocent people. They were Jews. To their last breaths they called out your name and prayed the Shema. They were murdered in your creation by your creatures. It is true we have killed each other and ignored your teachings. But you have watched and been quiet. You have observed and remained silent. You have seen and heard but you have not really seen and heard. When a mother watches her child running across a crowded street and the child is liable to be hurt by an oncoming vehicle, is not the mother morally obligated to act? Would that mother not be cruel to allow her child to be hit by a vehicle that the child might learn to listen to her teaching? If the mother would make such a claim, we would think her to be insane or immoral. How absurd to call such divine indifference justified!

"You say you are not responsible. You say we are the ones who have violated your laws. We have acted in this way because you have created us with these capacities. You have created us with varying moral potentials. We are after all, half human and half beast. Some of us, despite all the world's religions, the music, the art, the science, despite all the knowledge we have gained, have remained beasts. Indeed, less than beasts, for animals do not do what we have done to each other. What is inside us of us that you have created, which compels us to refuse to be tamed?"

The Lord replied to Job's words, "Job, you have spoken what is right. I confess I have evaded your questions as I did so many years ago. You are correct to press your case. The Lichtenfelds are dead and I refused to stop it. I watched and did not act. All the comforters and the 'friends' who speak today to defend and excuse my behavior are merely creating a god in their own image. All their theological explanations and theories evade the truth you have spoken. But the

43

truth will not let them go. I am sorry and guilty as charged, for having believed in my most complex creation, the human being.

"In the beginning I hoped against hope the human heart could be trained to be kind and compassionate. I hoped humanity's capacity for evil could be tamed. I wanted every man and woman to be a 'mensch.' I see now as I feared before the flood, the imagination of the human heart is perplexed and enchanted by evil. I had hoped my Torah could train humankind. I hoped all the Scriptures, hymns, creeds, doctrines, and rituals of every sort would transform them into human beings. It worked for some but not for too many. I was wrong. My attempt to influence them was insufficient. They failed. The killers kept on killing as if there was no God in their midst. The slaughter kept on despite all I had taught them. Job, on this count, you are right. I remained silent because I hoped against hope the human being could be made humane. I was wrong and I repent of such a misplaced hope."

And so God donned sackcloth and sat on the ashes, as Job once had, and lamented over what human beings had done, so much of it in God's name. Then, both God and Job arose, left the synagogue, and walked together through the village. It was too late for the Jews of Krasnobrod. Yet God and Job agreed to commit themselves to work together and do what they could do to resist the onslaught of human evil, to reform humanity despite humanity. But what could be done than had not been done? As they arrived at the mass graves outside of town, stared at the corpses, both wept and wondered if it was too late for the human being to be human.

From Text to Midrash to Text:
The Book of Job

"We don't know about God, but Jewish continuity was always paved with words."[3] "Ours is not a bloodline but a textline."[4] Jews have disagreed on so much over the years, but not about the importance and vitality of texts. Let's face it: God may or may not be real, but

---

3. Oz and Oz-Salzberger, *jews and words*, x.
4. Oz and Oz-Salzberger, *jews and words*, 1.

CHAPTER FOUR: THE BOOK OF JOB AND THE HOLOCAUST

the words in our texts are actual and they have given the divine life, energy, questions, and debates to Jews for generations.

What happens then to a biblical text when it passes through catastrophe? The text cannot remain untouched. It generates midrash in new interpretive contexts. The midrash above is an attempt to imagine what happens to a biblical text and its central character when he leaves his text and is compelled to walk through a small European town during the Holocaust. Every biblical text has intentional gaps for future readers to fill in as they wrestle with the text for their own time. The book of Job is no exception. It is a deeply probing work that contains gaps concerning the character and morality of God. God's response to Job in the final chapters of the book scarcely addresses Job's suffering or questions. Filling in the gaps becomes more urgent in this post-Holocaust age. This is precisely what Elie Wiesel did for the past fifty years. Rooted in the Scriptures and traditions of the Jewish people, he knew he could not ignore what had happened during those days. Much as he would have liked to continue to pray the old prayers endorsed by rabbinic tradition, he was compelled to persistently confront God with what happened during those days.

When Elie Wiesel examined biblical texts, he did so from a particular perspective. He believed we live today in the shadow of Auschwitz, a revelation of horrific evil. The word *Auschwitz* has become a metaphor for the mass extermination of one-third of the Jewish people over eighty years ago. For Wiesel, the event was revelatory, meaning all biblical texts must now pass through the gates of Auschwitz before we can listen to them anew. The journey for Job from the land of Uz to the village of Krasnobrod recasts the text. After Auschwitz Scripture is transformed. Nothing in Scripture can remain the same after it passes through the horror of the death camps. After Auschwitz, Scripture carries a much heavier burden than before. Whether it will be able to bear the crushing weight of such a dark revelation remains to be seen. Biblical texts for the most part suggest a powerful God working out his plans and purpose in human history. Auschwitz calls into question the character and morality of that God.

While the biblical text begins with a description of the man Job, the midrash begins with the village of Krasnobrod. Job is a visitor, an outsider, a non-Jew, and an observer. It is now Job, and not "the accuser" of the biblical tale, who roams the land inspecting what has happened. It is Job who will report to God what has occurred. No longer are Job's integrity and goodness described. Rather we hear of the innocence and fidelity of the Lichtenfelds. As in the biblical tale, Job accuses God of indifference and injustice in the presence of murdered children. The questions and accusations go on and on *ad nauseam*, as if there were not enough words to describe Job's anguish. After Auschwitz, Job is concerned not merely with God's compassion but more importantly with the justice of God. How can a loving, caring God watch the slaughter of innocent children and not be moved to act? What sort of love and justice is that? "God, are you there?" Is there a there there? Is there a God there? Can that God hear and see and know what is happening here; does God care, and can God do anything about it? These are the questions that have haunted human beings for millennia.

In the midrash, Job has no friends to console him. But Job does refer to comforters who have, throughout history, tried to exonerate and defend God by redefining either the omnipotence, goodness, or existence of God. He mentions those religious functionaries eager to offer apologies for God based on the mystery of God's providence or God's commitment to human free will, or God's suffering with the victims. Job declares all such defenses as inadequate attempts to get God off the hook. For Job and Wiesel, such explanations betray both God and the victims. There are no explanations that can adequately defend divine indifference. Job's charge is: God does not act like God!

As in the biblical text, God answers Job. This time the answer is not about the majesty of God's creation. After Auschwitz, creation can never be "good" again. Instead, God accuses human beings of moral depravity. Humans, God charges, have not acted according to divine instructions meted out to them in the distinct revelation of the Torah. God has given human beings certain teachings by which

CHAPTER FOUR: THE BOOK OF JOB AND THE HOLOCAUST

to live. Yet they have ignored God's words and are now receiving the just and due consequences of their acts.

In the biblical story, Job submits after God speaks. Job is repentant. God is right. Job confesses he is wrong: "I know that you can do all things, that no purpose of yours can be thwarted. Therefore I have uttered what I did not understand, things too wonderful for me, which I did not know" (Job 42:1-3).

But in the midrash Auschwitz has changed everything. Job will not tolerate any theological double talk, from God or from anyone else. What Job has seen cannot be unseen. He will not again allow God to evade the real question. Never mind what humans have done to disobey God. The true question is "Where was God when the Lichtenfelds of Krasnobrod were being murdered?" How were God's eyes able to endure the sight? What went through the divine mind as the children were being mercilessly shot to death?

More than anything Job speaks of God's memory. Throughout Scripture, God is depicted as one who remembers and thereby enacts covenants and promises made to individuals, communities, and creation. Job, too, remembers; he cannot and will not forget the death of his own children nor his wife's grieving. Having mentioned his own haunted memory, Job enquires about God's memory. Job is aware of the distance between the human and the divine. He wonders if God remembers the way we do. What happens to and within the divine memory after it experiences the death of a million and a half children? How does their blood compare to the blood of Abel? How is God affected by the shedding of all this blood?

In the biblical text, God, appearing out of the whirlwind, never answered Job's questions. In the midrash, God responds by confessing he has evaded Job's questions. God confesses to being silent while the Lichtenfelds were exterminated. God expresses remorse and speaks candidly of the failure of his teachings to be effective.

God had given the Torah that human beings might be truly human, and thus humane. To be truly human is to be a mensch. Mensch is a Yiddish word for someone who trusts God, resists the evil within and outside, and struggles to remain, despite every temptation, a person of character. Many humans have refused to be trained and restrained, and God is shocked at their refusal. And as in the biblical book, Job is told he was right in his speaking and his comforters were wrong (Job 42:7). "Comforters" in both the Bible and the midrash offer their explanations to evade the truth that Job has come to know so well—God is morally culpable for evil. The Job of the midrash faces up to this awful truth. In Krasnobrod, Job has gained the wisdom and courage he lacked in the land of Uz.

In Krasnobrod, something radically new occurs. God does not remain aloof from the reality of suffering, as in the biblical tale. Neither is Job rewarded with family and material things as at the end of the biblical book. The calamity of Auschwitz forces God down from the heavens. God and Job walk through the streets of Krasnobrod together. They walk by the graves of the murdered children. Both God and Job are keenly aware that each was silent when the Lichtenfelds were killed. In the presence of the victims, neither God nor human beings can ever be completely innocent. God and Job must forgive each other to remain sane before such absurd shocking evil. Each must now accompany the other. Henceforth, God and human beings inextricably walk together; weep together, seek to create order out of chaos, and most importantly resist together the craziness of evil. God and Job are now co-resisters of evil. As in the community lament prayers, their fates are inextricably conjoined, and they hope it is not too late.

The Holocaust is an event of such magnitude that all Scripture must be reinterpreted through that event. Why the Holocaust? Why should this one event be the interpretive lens through which we must come to understand the Scriptures for our age? Throughout history, human beings have interpreted certain events as paradigms, even revelations for reaching new understandings of the nature of reality. What these events have in common is that each occurred at such a significant time and with such compelling force that human beings were forced to rethink who they were and what gave meaning to their lives. In the Bible, Sinai and the Babylonian exile were two such events. Auschwitz,

CHAPTER FOUR: THE BOOK OF JOB AND THE HOLOCAUST

Elie Wiesel asserts, is our time's revelation. The power of these events lies in their capacity to call into question long-standing religious and cultural monuments of the past.

For a significant number of human beings, the old order will no longer work. After the Holocaust, the old words and stories that proclaim God's control over evil ring hollow. After the systematic mass murder of six million Jews, a million and a half children under the age of ten, how does one speak with integrity of a redeemed world? Indeed, it seems too late for messiahs or redeemers. Still, human beings must have order. When the old structures no longer work, new ones or variations of the old ones must be constructed or imagined. For Elie Wiesel, the event named Auschwitz was of such a magnitude that it compels the honest interpreter to search for a new understanding of God and the world.

The Holocaust is a revelatory event that should compel Jews, Christians, and Muslims to open their collective eyes to the failure of God to be God, as traditionally understood. Certain adherents of these traditions will deny and feel threatened by talk of God's failure. But those who dare to look squarely in the faces of the murdered children will know what has happened. For these interpreters, Auschwitz provides an unavoidable and necessary lens through which we must reread our Scriptures and religious traditions. The midrash presented above is but one attempt to look at one text through that lens. After the Holocaust, the Scriptures are no longer the same. After the Holocaust, being Jewish or Christian or Muslim can no longer be the same. After the Holocaust, God and Job are no longer the same. After the Holocaust, not one of us can remain the same!

Chapter Five: *Elie Wiesel and the Problem of God*

Night, Ani Maamin, and
The Trial of God

T he word *God* is problematic from the start. After all, where did this word *God* come from? Who invented it? What do we mean when we say this word? *God* was a word invented by humans to speak about ultimate energy and purposive meaning within the universe. A person who talks about God is called a theologian. A true theologian knows that he or she does not know what they are talking about. God is inherently a mystery. If there is an ultimate meaning to our existence, we have named it God. What can such a word mean in our secular, modern, scientific, technological, computerized lives? Some parts of our Jewish, Christian, and Islamic traditions speak about God as being an omnipotent, omniscient, and omnipresent being who created the universe. This being, so some parts of the traditions assert, has a mysterious plan and purpose for the history of his creation, indecipherable and unknowable by humans.

But, for many in our world today, God has become a superstitious relic of the past. Contemporary atheists and agnostics inform us: suffering and evil happen as a matter of chance and fortune; there is no God and only the fearful and ignorant continue to

CHAPTER FIVE: ELIE WIESEL AND THE PROBLEM OF GOD

believe. Decades ago, Freud declared we humans had invented God and had forgotten we did so. Many have assumed this assessment of the deity to be part of the modern view of God. This view of God came about because the traditional religious ways of talking about God no longer worked on the ground. The assumption at work in our modern way of thinking is: God worked for many centuries until the advent of science when God was essentially replaced by scientific theories that seemed to explain the universe and our existence in it with more adequacy.[1]

But here is the thing. It is my contention God has always been a problem. I use the word *problem* rather than *mystery* because the word *mystery* assumes knowledge beyond our ability to comprehend. Adherents of the word *mystery* would assert God's ways are not our ways. They would say, do not even attempt to enter the realm of mystery. Merely confess it as beyond your ability, live with faith in the methodology and mystery that is God. Some would argue to attempt to enter the realm of God's mysteries is an act of arrogant pride.

But the word *problem* opens the divine realm to theological enquiry and questions. As one who likes the word *problem*, I am convinced God is not frightened of our questions or puzzlement. God is aware God is a problem and expects us to struggle with God's methods. My point is that when we study the Scriptures, we discover God has always been a problem for human beings. God has always been difficult to understand. Contemporary atheists have not discovered anything new. If God was invented to cause human beings to not fear, God has not worked very well. Our human brains seem to contain plenty of fear and anxiety, God notwithstanding.

The lament prayers in the Bible bear witness to the fact God has always been confusing, contradictory, ambiguous, unreliable, and worst of all invisible. Jewish tradition has always contained a minority tradition that embraced questioning the methodology, justice, and rationale of God. Since it was believed God created

---

1. See Luhrmann, *How God Becomes Real*, for an anthropological discussion of the way human beings through imagination make God real.

human beings and had chosen to be in relationship with the Jewish people, God has invited and opened himself to questioning and argument. When Elie Wiesel encountered the horrific events of the Holocaust, he was not shy to declare God to be a problem. For Wiesel, Auschwitz was problematic with God. But without God, Auschwitz was catastrophic. Following a tradition thousands of years old, Wiesel hurled questions and accusations at God not as an act of unbelief but as an act of faith in a problematic God. We must still pursue this question: if God is so problematic, why do some people continue to trust in this enigmatic God?

From all of Elie Wiesel's works the three books which best exhibit the problem of God are *Night*, *Ani Maamin*, and *The Trial of God*. In this chapter we will examine the ways God is portrayed in these books and the problematic character of God now and always.

In his most popular work, *Night*, Elie Wiesel explains how a young Jewish boy from a small shtetel (town or village) named Sighet, in Romania, well-rooted in Jewish mystical tradition, came to experience the Holocaust. Wiesel begins his work by telling us about his teacher, Moshe, in those days. Moshe teaches Wiesel, "With great insistence that every question possessed a power that did not lie in the answer." Moshe goes on, "Man raises himself toward God by the questions he asks Him, that is the true dialogue. Man questions God and God answers. But we don't understand his answers. We can't understand them. Because they come from the depths of the soul, and they stay there until death."[2] Moshe asserts, "I pray to God within me that he will give me the strength to ask him the right questions." And Wiesel tells us, Moshe the Beadle would "draw me with him into eternity, into that time where question and answer would become one."[3]

As the Hungarian police urge and shove people into the ghetto, Wiesel prays, "Oh God, Lord of the universe, take pity upon us in Thy great mercy . . ."[4] After arriving in Auschwitz, and experiencing the burning of young children, Wiesel tells us,

---

2. Wiesel, *Night*, 14.
3. Wiesel, *Night*, 14.
4. Wiesel, *Night*, 29.

CHAPTER FIVE: ELIE WIESEL AND THE PROBLEM OF GOD

"Around us, everyone was weeping. Someone began to recite the Kaddish, the prayer for the dead. I do not know if it has ever happened before, in the long history of the Jews, that people have ever recited the prayer for the dead for themselves."[5] Then Wiesel adds, "For the first time, I felt revolt rise up in me. Why should I bless his name? The Eternal, Lord of the universe, the All-Powerful and Terrible, was silent. What had I to thank him for?"[6] And then Wiesel talks about the burning children:

> Never shall I forget that night, the first night in camp, which has turned my life into one long night, seven times cursed and seven times sealed. Never shall I forget that smoke. Never shall I forget the little faces of the children, whose bodies I saw turned into wreaths of smoke beneath a silent blue sky.
>
> Never shall I forget those flames which consumed my faith forever.
>
> Never shall I forget the nocturnal silence which deprived me, for all eternity, of the desire to live. Never shall I forget those moments which murdered my God and my soul and turned my dreams to dust. Never shall I forget these things, even if I am condemned to live as long as God Himself. Never.[7]

A few pages later, Wiesel tells us, "The student of the Talmud, the child that I was, had been consumed in the flames."[8] And still later on he says, "Some talked of God, of his mysterious ways, of the sins of the Jewish people, and of their future deliverance. But I had ceased to pray. How I sympathized with Job! I did not deny God's existence, but I doubted His absolute justice."[9]

Perhaps the most famous of Wiesel's recollections is the tale of two men and a young boy being hung.

---

5. Wiesel, *Night*, 43.
6. Wiesel, *Night*, 43.
7. Wiesel, *Night*, 44.
8. Wiesel, *Night*, 47.
9. Wiesel, *Night*, 56.

The three necks were placed at the same moment within the nooses.

"Long live liberty!" cried the two adults. But the child was silent. "Where is God? Where is He?" someone behind me asked.

At a sign from the head of the camp, the three chairs tipped over. Total silence throughout the camp. On the horizon the sun was setting.

"Bare your heads!" yelled the head of the camp. His voice was raucous. We were weeping.

Then the march past began. The two adults were no longer alive. Their tongues hung swollen, blue tinged. But the third rope was still moving; being so light, the child was still alive. . . .

For more than half an hour he stayed there, struggling between life and death, dying in slow agony under our eyes. And we had to look him full in the face. He was still alive when I passed in front of him. His tongue was red, his eyes not yet glazed.

Behind me, I heard the same man asking:

"Where is God now?"

And I heard a voice within me answer him:

"Where is he? Here he is, he is hanging here on this gallows . . ."

That night the soup tasted of corpses.[10]

On the eve of the Jewish holiday Rosh Hashanah (the Jewish New Year), Wiesel speaks of his wrestling with God. "What are you, my God, I thought angrily, compared to this afflicted crowd, proclaiming to You their faith, their anger, their revolt? What does your greatness mean, Lord of the Universe, in the face of all this weakness, this decomposition, and this decay? Why do you trouble

---

10. Wiesel, *Night*, 76.

their sick minds, their crippled bodies?"[11] Wiesel goes on: "Ten thousand men had come to attend the solemn service, heads of the blocks, Kapos, functionaries of death." As the multitude of Jews began to bless God, Wiesel said no! "Why, but why should I bless him? In every fiber I rebelled. Because He had thousands of children burned in his pits? Because He kept six crematories working night and day, on Sundays and feast days? Because in His great might He had created Auschwitz, Birkenau, Buna, and so many factories of death? How could I say to Him: "Blessed are Thou, Eternal, Master of the Universe, who chose us from among the races to be tortured day and night, to see our fathers, our mothers, our brothers, end in the crematory? Praised be Thy Holy Name, Thou who hast chosen us to be butchered on Thine altar?"[12] Wiesel adds the following frighteningly powerful lament:

> Yes, man is very strong, greater than God. When You were deceived by Adam and Eve, You drove them out of paradise. When Noah's generation displeased You, You brought down the Flood. When Sodom no longer found favor in Your eyes, You made the sky rain down fire and sulphur. But these men here, whom You have betrayed, whom you have allowed to be tortured, butchered, gassed, burned, what do they do? They pray before You! They praise Your name?
>
> This day I had ceased to plead. I was no longer capable of lamentation. On the contrary, I felt very strong. I was the accuser, God the accused. My eyes were open and I was alone—terribly alone in a world without God and without man. Without love or mercy. I had ceased to be anything but ashes, yet I felt myself to be stronger than the Almighty, to whom my life had been tied for so long. I stood amid that praying congregation, observing it like a stranger.[13]

11. Wiesel, *Night*, 77.
12. Wiesel, *Night*, 78.
13. Wiesel, *Night*, 79.

Finally, on the holy Jewish holiday of Yom Kippur, when Jews are required to fast and ask for God's forgiveness, Wiesel writes:

> I did not fast, mainly to please my father, who had forbidden me to do so. But further, there was no longer any reason why I should fast. I no longer accepted God's silence. As I swallowed my bowl of soup, I saw in the gesture an act of rebellion and protest against Him. And I nibbled my crust of bread. In the depths of my heart, I felt a great void.[14]

Through these words Wiesel refuses to lie. God had become problematic and Wiesel could no longer pretend. To respect the integrity of his faith meant to accuse God of having abandoned his people!

And Wiesel was not alone. In *Night*, he tells us about a man named Akiba Drumer. "I knew a rabbi from a little town in Poland, a bent old man, whose lips were always trembling. He used to pray all the time, in the block, in the yard, in the ranks. He would recite whole pages of the Talmud from memory, argue with himself, ask questions, and answer himself. And one day he said to me: 'it's the end. God is no longer with us.'" Wiesel quotes Rabbi Drumer: "I know. One has no right to say things like that. I know. Man is too small, too humble and inconsiderate to seek to understand the mysterious ways of God. But what can I do? I'm not a sage, one of the elect, nor a saint. I'm just an ordinary creature of flesh and blood. I've got eyes, too, and I can see what they're doing here. Where is the divine mercy? Where is God? How can I believe, how could anyone believe, in this merciful God?"[15]

And yet, when Wiesel witnessed a son abandoning his father, Wiesel wrote this: "And in spite of myself, a prayer rose in my heart, to that God in whom I no longer believed. My God, Lord of the Universe, give me strength never to do what Rabbi Eliahou's son has done."[16]

---

14. Wiesel, *Night*, 80.
15. Wiesel, *Night*, 87.
16. Wiesel, *Night*, 104.

CHAPTER FIVE: ELIE WIESEL AND THE PROBLEM OF GOD

Reflections on *Night*

Elie Wiesel wrote over fifty-three books, gave many lectures, wrote many articles. Everything he said and wrote was a reflection on the book *Night* and his experience in the camps. He wrote as a witness to those days. Throughout his life, Wiesel pondered and struggled with the problem of God. After reading *Night*, the reader might wonder, did Wiesel lose his faith while a prisoner in the camps? Yes and no. Yes, his childish, naïve faith in a God who would rescue the Jewish people died. But he continued to believe God existed while also continuing to doubt God's justice. In the camps, he had seen too much and had experienced all that there was to experience in the hell the Nazis created.

I have read and reread *Night* many times, haunted by its sadness and truth. I too, as a child, and even as an adult, wanted God to be a God who operated like Superman. In my romantic religious naivete I wanted a God who watched over me and when trouble, pain, or better yet, evil, came would be there to halt its advance. This was an expectation given to me by the rabbis I met early in my life, attending Yeshiva. I was taught good and evil came from God. If we did not understand why things happened the way they did, that was our problem, our inability to understand the mystery of the divine plan and purpose. Such beliefs work until they stop working. The old beliefs stopped working for Elie Wiesel in the camps in those days. And he spent his life trying to figure out what it all meant. The old beliefs have stopped working for me as well because when I read Wiesel his words rang of truth.

When I say my beliefs "stopped working" I mean we all have certain understandings of how the universe works. These beliefs may contain a certain inconsistent mixture of religious, scientific, technological beliefs. When we open our eyes at the beginning of the day we step out of bed without a thought because we know the floor is there. Our beliefs about the way the world works is that floor. But when those beliefs are contradicted by the reality we are experiencing, we can no longer trust the floor is there or stable. We become disoriented and this disorientation results in a kind of madness. We struggle to create or figure out a new orientation, a new floor upon which we can walk without fear.

The frightening part of *Night* is it leaves us without a floor. When we finish the book, we are left with Wiesel looking in a mirror and discovering a corpse staring back at him. What do we do with that picture? We are left living in a world "without God and without man." And this is our dilemma. How can we keep talking about such a problematic God in such a perplexing world without throwing our brains in the toilet? Let's be honest. Wiesel's books unintentionally have the potential to turn us all into practical atheists. In Wiesel's writings certain images of God die. And we are left to wonder what we are to do now. Should we invent new images of God that work even in Auschwitz? Should we redefine, rethink, reconceive, reappropriate, until we each find our own image of God?

In the end, I think we are better off living with Wiesel's unanswered questions. Why so? Because if there is a God, he, she, or it needs to act like a God. It is not difficult to create a less powerful God and declare him to be God. But to me that is another form of idolatry. Either with Wiesel we let God be God or we give up on God entirely. But how many people are willing to live with Wiesel's questions, accusations, and his argument with God? What good can come from questioning a silent God? Doesn't such questioning destroy faith? The real question is, does screaming or arguing with God have any effect? Does it change anything?

Ani Maamin

Ani Maamin, in Hebrew, means "I believe." In 1973, Elie Wiesel wrote this song, legend, parable, or better, cantata, in which he asserted this statement of faith: "I believe in the coming of the Messiah and though he tarry I shall wait, I shall wait, I shall wait." Throughout his life Wiesel remained a religious person who trusted in God despite, in spite, and to spite the one he called God. In that vein he wrote this poem, *Ani Maamin*, in which the three holiest men in Jewish history, the founding fathers, Abraham, Isaac, and Jacob, during the Holocaust, approach God to convince the

CHAPTER FIVE: ELIE WIESEL AND THE PROBLEM OF GOD

deity to act. As we have seen, the idea that God could be moved to act by appeals to his promises to his people is rooted in the biblical laments. The cantata begins with a disconcerting preface:

> Ani maamin beviat ha-Mashiah, I believe in the coming of the Messiah. One of the thirteen Articles of Faith set forth by Maimonides, it was also the song transformed into a hymn by pious and obstinate Jews in the ghettos and camps. Rather than appeasing, rather than consoling the survivors, this faith disconcerts them. Both affirmation and provocation, it cannot help but evoke uneasiness. And yet . . .[17]

In the opening appeal of the cantata, the chorus asserts the ancient faith that God will soon send the Messiah, and then says, "Be worthy of it, O Lord. Be worthy of us, O Savior. Ani maamin, ani maamin. For you, O Lord. With you. In you. Against you. Ani maamin, ani maamin. Hear us, O God, hear us."[18]

The narrator then tells us: "In those days, even as the heart of the world was being consumed by the black flames of night, three angry old men appeared before the celestial court, asking to be heard. Abraham, Isaac, and Jacob—the three forefathers of a people consecrated to God by God—were desperate. Their mission had been to roam the by-roads near and far, gathering the echoes of Jewish suffering in the world, and make them known in heaven. They wanted to bring it to an end."[19] They wanted to convince God to act.

> For their mission overwhelmed them. Wherever their eyes had wandered, they had beheld agony and humiliation. Communities of uprooted families buried alive. Men and women, the children and the sick, the wise and the insane, insane with sorrow and silence, the rich and the poor, speaking every tongue, come from every corner of the world: all swept away by the storm.

---

17. Wiesel, *Ani Maamin*, 11.
18. Wiesel, *Ani Maamin*, 15.
19. Wiesel, *Ani Maamin*, 15.

Abraham, Isaac and Jacob felt guilty, guilty of having seen, guilty of being helpless.[20]

First comes Abraham: Abraham reminds God how he first came to know and trust God. Then he says, "As a reward, you promised me: My children and my children's children would live, Would grow and bless us, you and me, you promised us survival, Not just eternity. Well, Master of the Universe, Behold! Open your eyes and see!"[21] Isaac is next: Isaac reminds God of the "Akeda," the (near) sacrifice on Mount Moriah and speaks of his faithfulness to God despite what was happening to him. And Isaac asserts, "Do you see what I have seen below? Behold God of Abraham, God of mercy, Open your eyes as you have opened mine, Open your eyes and see what I have seen."[22] And finally Jacob, the ancient dreamer of dreams, reminds God, "You promised so many things, my Lord. You promised me to watch over Israel. Where are you? What of your promise? You promised me blessings for Israel. Is this your blessing? Behold, O Lord: Esau is winning the battle. Is this your victory as well?"[23] The narrator tells us: "And Jacob began to weep. And so did Abraham. And Isaac. And all the angels, all the seraphim from all the heavens joined in their weeping. But not God. He alone remained calm. Unmoved. Silent."[24] A few pages later the narrator tells us about the flames: "Flames—never before have there been such flames. And on every one of them it is the vision of the Redeemer that is dying—never before has hope been murdered so. The witnesses testify and the celestial tribunal listens in silence. The supreme judges say nothing while an entire people enters night, plunges into the divine abyss—an abyss inhabited by God

20. Wiesel, *Ani Maamin*, 15.
21. Wiesel, *Ani Maamin*, 19.
22. Wiesel, *Ani Maamin*, 23.
23. Wiesel, *Ani Maamin*, 25.
24. Wiesel, *Ani Maamin*, 25.

CHAPTER FIVE: ELIE WIESEL AND THE PROBLEM OF GOD

alone."[25] And still later the narrator tells us, "It is the Bible that is being killed, the prophets that are being massacred."[26]

The cantata continues with Abraham, Isaac, and Jacob working diligently to make God aware of what is happening to God's people. They keep telling God they do not understand. They are afraid. They are afraid to understand. The chorus implores God: "Hear, O God, O God, answer. On behalf of Abraham, Isaac, and Jacob, on behalf of your defenders your children implore you: Hear and answer!" And the narrator tells us: "But heaven is silent, and its silence is a wall."[27] Yet the narrator perseveres despite the silence. Addressing God, he says:

> Abraham looked: do as he did. Isaac looked: do as he did. Jacob looked: weep as he wept. Warsaw, Bialystok, Theresienstadt: stained stars, stained with blood, stained with soot. Lodz, Kiev, Satmar. Minsk, Lublin, Transnistrea: mass graves, rivers of life, rivers of death. Winds of rage, peaks of hate. How many victims? A thousand times a thousand—and more. A thousand times a thousand mothers—and more—in a barren universe. Creator of the Universe, that is your creation.

On and on and on the attempt to awaken God proceeds: "Look at the children, Look at their faces, Look at them well, They fill the world. Invaded, the heavens. Invaded the source. Invaded, too, your eyes. These children have taken your countenance, O God."[28] How can God look at what is happening and be still? The chorus exclaims: "God is silent, God looks on. God is, is the look. God looks, looks at God."[29] Despite the importunity of the three old angry men the narrator informs us:

> Meanwhile the story goes on. The torturers go on torturing, the soldiers go on shooting. The victims, spurning the cemeteries, rise to the highest palace, if not higher.

25. Wiesel, *Ani Maamin*, 29.
26. Wiesel, *Ani Maamin*, 35.
27. Wiesel, *Ani Maamin*, 47.
28. Wiesel, *Ani Maamin*, 57.
29. Wiesel, *Ani Maamin*, 57.

Below, there are no more cemeteries. Our cemetery is in heaven. And so the three patriarchs in powerful unison, ask God the most human of questions, the most terrifying, too: Why? Why, O Lord? O Father, why?[30]

Finally, a voice is heard from heaven: "Unfathomable, The divine thought. Blind, Man plunges into it. Unknowing of its outcome. God knows What he is doing—For man. That must suffice."[31] Suddenly an argument breaks out between the voice from heaven and Abraham. The voice assures Abraham that everything that happens is under God's purview. The Messiah will come in due time. Abraham answers, "But what kind of messiah, is it a messiah who demands Six million dead before he reveals himself?" The voice responds, "God knows, that is enough. God wills, that is enough. God takes and God gives back. And that is enough. God breaks and God consoles, that is enough." Abraham is furious!

> No. it is not enough! God is consolation? Who says so? He? Or I? Not enough! The victims are not saying it! Never will the hearts of my descendants Be consoled! Never will the wound Be healed, Nor the shame Erased. Never will our mourning be assuaged—never![32]

The voice hollers back:

> Desist! What do you want? What do you seek to prove? Accomplish? What right have you to speak? To speak thus? Does God owe you an accounting? God alone? All this—His sole responsibility? What about man? What about his role? Does God not have the right to question you, in turn, to ask of man: What have you done with my creation?[33]

The narrator interrupts the argument to let us know,

> Suddenly Abraham, Isaac and Jacob are at a loss, conscious of the futility of their efforts. God chooses to be

---

30. Wiesel, *Ani Maamin*, 61.
31. Wiesel, *Ani Maamin*, 67.
32. Wiesel, *Ani Maamin*, 72.
33. Wiesel, *Ani Maamin*, 75.

CHAPTER FIVE: ELIE WIESEL AND THE PROBLEM OF GOD

question. The answer is not known. Nor will it be. Know it only those who, from Babi-Yar to Treblinka, fled the earth, fled from life and they are mute. Like God. And here they are, crushed, more than ever. Abraham, Isaac and Jacob. For now it is clear: God knows—and remains silent. God knows—so it must be his will. The Jewish people of the black era—doomed by God. The Jewish people of tomorrow will live, live again. Perhaps know glory and joy. And yet the scandal will remain.[34]

The three patriarchs conclude they need to go tell the victims there is no hope. But unbeknownst to all, the narrator tells us: "Having spoken, Abraham takes another step backward. He does not, cannot, see that God for the first time permits a tear to cloud his eyes."[35] Isaac speaks, "Ani maamin, I believe in God. With the last of my strength I claim him as my own, Ani maamin, I believe in the coming of the Messiah, though he may be late, Though God may be unwilling."[36] And the narrator informs us, "for the second time a tear streams down God's somber countenance, a countenance more somber than before."[37] Jacob gives a lengthy speech that he concludes by saying, "Auschwitz has killed Jews but not their expectation." And once again the narrator lets us know, "Having spoken, Jacob withdraws, and does not, cannot, see that God surprised by his people weeps for the third time—and this time without restraint, and with—yes—love. He weeps over his creation—and perhaps over much more than his creation."[38] Abraham comments, "May you be blessed Israel For your faith in God, in spite of God."[39]

And for the last time the narrator tells us: "Abraham, Isaac and Jacob go away, heartened by another hope: their children. They leave heaven and do not, cannot, see that they are no longer alone:

34. Wiesel, *Ani Maamin*, 75.
35. Wiesel, *Ani Maamin*, 93.
36. Wiesel, *Ani Maamin*, 95.
37. Wiesel, *Ani Maamin*, 96–97.
38. Wiesel, *Ani Maamin*, 103.
39. Wiesel, *Ani Maamin*, 103.

God accompanies them, weeping, smiling, whispering, *Nitzhuni banai,* my children have defeated me, they deserve my gratitude. Thus he spake—he is speaking still. The word of God continues to be heard. So does the silence of his dead children."⁴⁰

The cantata concludes with the chorus singing Ani Maamin:

> Ani maamin, Abraham, Despite Treblinka, Ani maamin, Isaac, Because of Belsen. Ani maamin, Jacob, because and in spite of Majdanek. Dead in vain, dead for naught, Ani maamin. Pray men. Pray to God, Against God, For God, Ani maamin. Whether the Messiah comes, Ani maamin. Or is late in coming, Ani maamin, Whether God is silent or weeps, Ani maamin. Ani maamin for him, in spite of him. I believe in you, even against your will. Even if you punish me for believing in you. Blessed are the fools Who shout their faith. Blessed are the fools Who go on laughing, who mock the man who mocks the Jew, who help their brothers singing over and over: Ani Maamin.⁴¹

Reflections on *Ani Maamin*

From the biblical lament prayers to the words of *Ani Maamin,* we can draw a few theological conclusions. First, arguing with God is part and parcel of what it means to be Jewish. Such arguing comes from within faith, is part of faith, and at the heart of faith. Second, God is willing to engage with and approves of such arguing. Third, sometimes people are called to trust in God despite God's silence, in spite of God's silence, to spite God, in and within God's silence. Fourth, for all the laments and arguing with God, these prayers may not move God to act.

What can we moderns say about all this? For those of us who want to keep on with God, we must confess: Faith is trusting without knowing for sure. Despite all that Wiesel experienced in the camps, he was not prepared to give up on God. Because of his

---

40. Wiesel, *Ani Maamin,* 105.
41. Wiesel, *Ani Maamin,* 107.

CHAPTER FIVE: ELIE WIESEL AND THE PROBLEM OF GOD

religious history he was determined to live in the tension between doubting, questioning, accusing, and arguing with God while continuing to believe God would yet act like God. Living in such a tension is not easy, not to mention intellectually and theologically problematic, but such is the character of Wiesel's faith and my own. We moderns who trust our five senses find it difficult to live in such theological tension. Many would rather reject any notion of God and will not try to live in Wiesel's tension. Others choose to ignore the problem and keep on praising or making excuses for God. But I would assert, after Auschwitz, there may be no other honest way of speaking about the traditional deity except as Wiesel does. It may be the only way to continue to take the deity and our faith seriously.

But here is the point: This has always been the situation of observant Jews and other believers. From biblical times until today, God has been a problem. God's methodology is problematic. God does not always play fair. If you want to have faith, know that faith is always caught in Wiesel's theological tension. No matter how we want to twist our understanding of God, we are grasped by the questions and they will not let us go. So it was then and so it is now. God remains a problem. Did the three patriarchs confront God with the Holocaust? Did it really happen? Does it matter? The fact is: whether God exists or does not exist, God remains a problem. And the questions or laments we address to God may be more real than God himself. And the fact is: even when God does not answer, God's silence and absence is real.

Let us continue to examine Wiesel's paradoxical religious tension in its boldest form through his play, *The Trial of God*, written in 1979.

The Trial of God

The Trial of God is a play and a cantata. On the surface, it is not about God and the Holocaust, but of course, that is precisely what it is about. In Auschwitz, Wiesel witnessed a trial of God. He said he intended the play as a farce, but it is far from that. The play begins with Purim. Purim is a Jewish holiday rooted in the book of Esther. And Esther is a book in the Bible which does not mention the name of God. Esther is a book in which the Jews are ultimately saved by the wisdom and creativity of Mordechai and Esther over the evil Haman. Haman, an assistant to the king, had planned to murder all the Jews in the kingdom. In the end Haman is killed on the very day he had planned to murder the Jews. Purim is a holiday that many Jews celebrate by drinking and dancing in memory of the victory gained in the biblical book. They also put on plays or purimschpiel on this holiday when everything is turned upside down.

In Wiesel's play, it is Purim, February 25, 1649, in the town of Shamgorod; the play begins in a tavern in this small village. Three players or purimschpieler who are lost happen to arrive in the town of Shamgorod. They sit in the tavern and demand something to drink while they converse with the owner, Berish. Berish seems angry and skeptical. And soon they find out why. The town has just been through a pogrom. A pogrom is a violent attack by the residents of a town on their Jewish neighbors. The only Jews left after the pogrom are the innkeeper and his daughter, who was raped during her wedding. Berish convinces the players to put on a play in which God is put on trial. Berish is angry at God for having not interfered as the Jews of the town were massacred. They all agree to hold a trial since it is Purim. Berish will be the prosecutor. But who will be the defense attorney? A strange visitor appears named Sam, who volunteers for the job.

One of the purimschpieler announces they have come to Shamgorod to put on a play for the Jewish community. Berish is amazed at this proposal since there is no longer a Jewish community. The actors discover there has been a pogrom. Mendel, one of the play actors, asks Berish if he prays. He answers, "Why do you ask? Why do you want to know? What business is it of yours whether I pray or not?"[42] And later, Mendel asks Berish, "And God in all this, innkeeper? Tell me: Where is God in all this?" Berish explodes: "What do you want from me? Am I his keeper? I

---

42. Wiesel, *Trial of God*, 13.

CHAPTER FIVE: ELIE WIESEL AND THE PROBLEM OF GOD

resigned from membership in God—I resigned from God. Let him look for another innkeeper, let him find another people, let him push around another Jew—I'm through with him!"[43]

The trial follows with Berish as the prosecuting attorney and Sam as the defense lawyer. Here is a bit of their argument about the justice of God.

Berish: "I knew how to wait once... I waited and I waited for redemption and who do you think came? The redeemer? No: the killers. God sought me out and God struck me down. So let him stay away from me. His company is annoying me. He is unwelcome in my house. And in my life."[44] "I distrust miracles. They exist only in books, and books say anything."[45] Asked what his truth is, Berish responds, "I don't know what it is, but I know it is an angry truth! Yes, I am boiling with anger! Don't ask me why, you know why! If you don't, I do! But you do know why. You are in Shamgorod, you must know. To mention God's mercy in Shamgorod is an insult. Speak of his cruelty instead. You see what I mean?" "I want to understand why He is giving strength to the killers and nothing but tears and the shame of helplessness to the victims." "Because I would refuse to understand—I would refuse to understand so as not to forgive Him."[46] "It's stupid but I can't help it: before I hardly thought of Him; now I do—and I hate myself for it."[47] Berish offers this indictment of God:

> Men and women are being beaten, tortured and killed—how can one *not* be afraid of Him? True, they are victims of men. But the killers kill in His name. Not all? True, but numbers are unimportant. Let one killer kill for His glory, and He is guilty. Every man who suffers or causes suffering, every woman who is raped, every child who is tormented implicates Him. What, you need more? A hundred or a thousand? Listen: either He is responsible,

43. Wiesel, *Trial of God*, 15.
44. Wiesel, *Trial of God*, 26.
45. Wiesel, *Trial of God*, 40.
46. Wiesel, *Trial of God*, 43.
47. Wiesel, *Trial of God*, 45.

or He is not. If He is, let's judge him; if He is not, let Him stop judging us.[48]

In act three, Berish states his formal charges: "I—Berish, Jewish innkeeper at Shamgorod—accuse Him of hostility, cruelty and indifference. Either he dislikes His chosen people, or He doesn't care about them—period! But then why has He chosen us—why not someone else, for a change? Either He knows what is happening to us, or He doesn't wish to know! In both cases He is . . . He is . . . guilty! Yes, guilty!"[49]

Sam: "Oh, I do not dispute the events, but I consider them to be highly irrelevant to the case before us, your Honor. I do not deny that blood was shed and that life was extinguished, but I am asking the question: Who is to blame for all that? After all, the situation seems to be simple indeed: men and women and children were massacred by other men. Why involve, why implicate their Father in Heaven?"[50]

Berish: "You want to leave him out? Turn him into a neutral bystander? Would a father stand by quietly, silently, and watch his children being slaughtered?"

Sam: "When human beings kill one another, where is God to be found? You see Him among the killers. I find Him among the victims."

Berish: "He—a victim? A victim is powerless; is He powerless? He is almighty, isn't He? He could use his might to save the victim, but He doesn't! So—on whose side is He? Could the killer kill without His blessing—without His complicity?"[51]

For the rest of the cantata the back-and-forth continues with Berish charging God with complicity and indifference and Sam defending God with the traditional excuses offered for the silence of God. In fact, if you are a conservative religious person, at first you will sympathize with Sam's defense of God. You do not want

48. Wiesel, *Trial of God*, 54.
49. Wiesel, *Trial of God*, 125.
50. Wiesel, *Trial of God*, 128.
51. Wiesel, *Trial of God*, 128–29.

CHAPTER FIVE: ELIE WIESEL AND THE PROBLEM OF GOD

to blame or accuse God. Such talk has the feel of faithlessness. But as the play goes on Sam's identity is revealed. He is Satan. At the conclusion of the play, he laughs and says, "So, you took me for a saint, a Just? Me? How could you be that blind? How could you be that stupid? If you only knew, if you only knew..."[52]

Reflections on *The Trial of God*

Listening to the anger and rage of Berish directed at God, I could easily see reading this play and deciding to be an atheist. But I do not think that was what Elie Wiesel was after in writing this piece. Wiesel is aware of all the excuses given to support and defend the silence and indifference of God. He puts these apologetic words in Sam's mouth. Only Satan would try to defend God after such a catastrophe as the Holocaust. Continued faith in God requires charging God with doing wrong. And that is the heart of the play. Berish sees clearly what has happened. His eyes, like Wiesel's, have been opened wide. The people of God have been attacked and God stood by and let it happen. God is guilty of abandoning his people. Any defense of God is inherently demonic, evil, and blaspheming.

The anger and rage of Berish emanates from within the disappointment of his faith and trust in God. He feels betrayed by God, by the religious tradition, by the rabbis, by anyone who refuses to see what must be seen. Evil happened and God did not respond. That is a fact! There can be no moral defense.

The real question is, why does Wiesel continue with God? Assuming Berish is correct, and God is guilty as charged, why not just give up on God? I suspect it is because Wiesel is a traditional Jew, and he continues to hope God will yet act like God. He refuses to lie about what has happened and he will not defend God. God must be made to see what has happened. The truth must be hurled in God's face. Such honesty is not a sign of disrespect or lack of faith. On the contrary, it is the highest form of faith, to continue to hope against hope that God is at work in this world.

52. Wiesel, *Trial of God*, 161.

Elie Wiesel will not lie or be deceived. The truth must be spoken and he, Berish/Wiesel, tries to speak it.

I have used this play to raise the problem of God with many of my Christian students. While they seem to understand the anger and rage of Berish, they are perplexed at the notion of arguing with or accusing God. To many of them, God is love and they see themselves as saved by God's grace. To charge God with doing wrong is an act of unbelief. After I explained the Jewish tradition of arguing with God, they understood it but they did not get it. It just seemed so foreign to their religious training.

But let's be clear: the lament tradition, whether in the Hebrew Scriptures or in Jewish tradition, was always a minority tradition. The problem of God's methodology was a mystery and an embarrassment. Why God acted in such an inconsistent manner was never understood. While questioning, arguing with, and accusing God can be found in the tradition, it was not given a central or prominent place. If you attend today most contemporary Jewish synagogues you will probably not hear about the laments. Yet, they are part of the tradition without which the Holocaust cannot be encountered. Elie Wiesel is right to question the justice and the morality of God and no amount of theological or religious excuses and explanations defending God can silence the questions.

Chapter Six: *Why God Is a Problem*

The Christian Years

How did a young Jewish boy from the Bronx end up in Minot, North Dakota? On a beautiful spring day in 1966 when I was seventeen and one-half years old, my father escorted me to Fordham Road in the Bronx to an Air Force recruiting station, where the recruiter explained what it would mean if I enlisted in the Air Force. Our country was involved in the Vietnam War and the draft was a possibility for all young men. After high school I was not ready to attend college. I found school to be boring and tedious. And I was desperate to get away from the apartment of my parents. In November of 1966, I began three and one-half years of service in the Air Force. I was young and immature. It was the first time I had been so far away from home. The recruiter promised I would see the world, but I ended up being stationed in San Antonio, Texas, Biloxi, Mississippi, isolated Iceland, and finally two and one-half years in Minot, North Dakota.

For the first time, I was out of any kind of Jewish milieu. I was eating a variety of unkosher foods. I went out with Christian girls. I learned how to drive. I bought a car. I listened to music by Bob Dylan, Phil Ochs, and a host of anti-Vietnam War musicians who made me begin to wonder about the existence and justice of God. I met and befriended Christians and wondered what Christianity was all about. I was discovering the complicated religious nature of the world and had begun to question what it meant that I was Jewish. I trusted God in some sort of vague manner, but was young, naïve, and ignorant.

After I was discharged from the Air Force in 1970, I decided to attend North Dakota State University in Fargo. The university waived tuition for veterans and I was not eager to return to New York to live with my parents. I majored in history and minored in political science. I began to read books about the Holocaust. Up to that point I had not thought of myself as being a child of Holocaust survivors. I knew my parents had emigrated from Europe in the 1947 and I knew we did not have many relatives.

It was at this time I first read Elie Wiesel's *Night*.

It was also at this time I met a Christian girl who would become my first wife. She was a Lutheran. And as we became more serious and after I got up the courage to tell her I was Jewish, I attended church with her, went to some introductory classes, and eventually converted to Christianity mostly for the sake of convenience. I did not think I had thereby stopped being Jewish, but I knew this was a big step.

There is an old saying: "the convert sings loudest." I had converted but I did not know much about my newfound faith. After graduating from NDSU, I decided to attend a Lutheran seminary in St. Paul, Minnesota. I thought that if I became a minister, I could speak the truth in the tradition of Martin Luther King Jr., who had urged his followers "to live a committed life." It sounds naïve and self-serving now and it probably was then, but those were my thoughts at the time. After we married, we moved to Minnesota, and I began to find out about the nature, character, and theology of the Lutheran tradition.

I had many doubts. What had I gotten myself into? Maybe I should have gone after my PhD in history as I had originally planned? I attended classes at Luther Seminary, but I was full of misgivings and questions. The seminary was a good place to raise questions and wrestle with theological issues. During my first year at seminary, I visited rabbis in the St. Paul area. I drove to the

CHAPTER SIX: WHY GOD IS A PROBLEM

University of Minnesota and considered enrolling in their graduate history program. I was genuinely lost.

In the summer after my first year at Luther Seminary, I had the good fortune to meet a pastor named Don Burton, and worked with him in the summer of 1973 in Bismarck, North Dakota. Here was a pastor who encouraged and allowed me to raise my doubts and questions about Christianity. He shared some of his own concerns. He listened and wrestled with me through various theological issues. He taught me that being Christian did not mean having all the answers. And it was okay to have doubts and to struggle to figure out the truth. I returned to seminary, made good friends with other students, and had helpful discussions with some professors. After four years, when I finished seminary, I decided to become a parish pastor. I was convinced the parish was where the real work of being Christian worked itself out. Here I was: a Jewish boy from New York being ordained a Lutheran pastor. I still had my doubts and questions. I found myself caught between two traditions.

I accepted a call to a church in rural Minnesota, where I served for a little over two years. But something was wrong. I would stand in front of a congregation of Christians, make the sign of the cross, but I would feel guilty. I had run far away from my community and tradition, but still I was not at peace. At this time I interviewed at Augustana College in Sioux Falls for a two-year position teaching in their religion department. I was lucky to get the position because I did not have a terminal degree. In my first classes at Augustana, I began to teach Wiesel's *Night* and to grapple with my students concerning the justice of God during those days. I struggled to understand how it was possible for a loving God to watch what had happened in the Nazi camps and not be moved to intervene.

And so, in 1979 when Elie Wiesel came to our campus to speak, I was ready to hear his words, which would change my life and eventually cause me to leave the church and return to my community. I truly was an unconverted convert! I had converted but had never really become a believer. The fact was: I was Jewish and could not encounter the world through falsehood. I became

73

a Christian in 1971 and returned to the Jewish community and tradition in 2000.

We are alive at a time when many people have decided there is no God. Many have concluded the traditional images of God do not work. They have determined all of us on the planet have been left to live alone on this lonely sphere rotating in the universe. Many assert there is no meaning or purpose to our lives other than what each person decides for themselves. And what is right or wrong is up to each person to determined for themselves. For an increasing number, traditional religion is understood to be superstitious nonsense.

On the other hand, there are others who continue to believe and defend certain scriptural and traditional depictions of God. These people think of God as mysterious, inscrutable, all-powerful, omniscient, in control of history, the creator of good or evil. Some say God gave people freedom and that is why undeserved suffering and evil exist. These people assume God knows what God is doing and they believe they live and breathe by God's grace. To question or accuse God would be seen by some as an act of overweening pride or arrogant unbelief. The key for these people is faith. I get it. I've seen and heard it.

The problem is whether we are believers in God or not, we do not know what we are talking about when we say the word *God*. Who is this God you do not believe in and who is the God you are sure is real? When our Scriptures tell us about God, they use anthropomorphic and anthropopathic ways of talking about God. They do so in an attempt to understand. But if you take the Bible seriously you will see that there are contradictory images of God within the Scriptures. In Exodus, for example, God is pictured simultaneously as in control of history and out of control of history. God rescues the Israelites with unlimited power and strength but God is also pictured as being absent and silent when undeserved suffering and evil occurs.

The biblical tradition recognized God was a problem and was comfortable living with opposites. The opposites could not be separated if the truth was to be told. God was a paradox. As

CHAPTER SIX: WHY GOD IS A PROBLEM

much as some things seemed clear, other matters are puzzling and problematic. The biblical texts are aware of the tensions and refuse to lie or cover up the problem.

That is the genius of Wiesel's approach to God. He refuses to let God off the hook. And he will not lie about what he has seen.

According to the Jewish Scriptures, God made covenants with the Jewish people that involved certain obligations and responsibilities on both sides. As far as Wiesel can see, from the perspective of justice, God has failed to live up to agreements and morality God previously endorsed. But Wiesel will not give in to either extreme: He will not decide there is no God, and he will not conclude God is always right. He asserts his right to question and accuse God as an expression of his faith. How did Wiesel's views collide with my Christian faith?

From 1971 until the year 2000, I was a Lutheran Christian. What did I learn during those years? Many Christians talk about God. And many are convinced faith is at the heart of what it means to be Christian. This differs from Jews and Judaism. As an old rabbi taught me long ago: the key to understanding a person does not lie in the tongue but in the feet. If I want to know the nature and character of your belief, I will not listen to your mouth but follow your feet instead. For Jews the secret to life and God is in the doing. What you do determines who you are. For Jews, God does not care so much what you believe, God cares what you do. Jews may or may not have faith in God, but many continue to do what they can to live out the commandments of God. Jews do not so much talk about God as talk to God. They do not so much talk theology as they do theology. And the God Jews worship is not so much a God of love as Christians confess. The Jewish God is a God that cares about justice.

As I lived among Christians, I learned to be a Lutheran theologian. That means I talked about God through a particular Lutheran prism. I consistently tried to figure out how to mesh the Lutheran and Jewish approaches to God within my brain. To a certain extent this worked, but in the end it could not hold up.

75

There are three beliefs at the heart of what it means to be Lutheran, which originally came from the New Testament letter writer Paul, and then from Augustine, and then Martin Luther: *Sola fidei, sola gratia,* and *sola scriptura.* Lutherans see themselves as a movement in the church which emphasizes the grace of God. The great strength of Lutheran theology as I see it is its emphasis on the ambiguous, inconsistent, and unreliable nature of human beings. This is what Christians call our sinful condition. They believe the God who appeared on Mount Sinai came to this world in the Messiah Jesus. Lutherans believe in justification by grace through faith. This means that through the cross and resurrection of Jesus, God saves all human beings from the power of sin, death, and evil. How does that happen? Mysteriously, through the death of Jesus human sins are forgiven. Through Jesus' resurrection humans are promised death will not have the final word and they will all be raised. And, finally, though evil is real because of sin, we are never alone and nothing shall separate us from the love of God. If you should ask, "what is the will of God when it comes to the undeserved suffering and evil in our world," you would hear: Jesus is the will of God!

I also learned about the hidden and revealed God. God is a mysterious and inscrutable being. The heart of God, filled with mercy and forgiveness, is revealed through the cross. The will of God apart from the cross is hidden. Human attempts to get behind the curtain to see and understand the hiddenness or glory of God are acts of human arrogance and pride. A theology of the cross is contrasted with a theology of glory. Questioning the justice of God is permitted but not encouraged, since it detracts from faith. Besides which any question we might have will only catapult the person back to the promises of God articulated through the cross. Faith is trusting without knowing for sure. And faith which comes to us through God's grace is at the heart of the Lutheran tradition.

Lutheran theology is quite sophisticated and paradoxical. The event of the incarnation, God becoming human in Jesus, and the notion that Jesus is 100 percent human and 100 percent God are paradoxical truths. They may not make sense to our senses,

CHAPTER SIX: WHY GOD IS A PROBLEM

but are confessed as true. The same goes for the Trinity, God being present as Father, Son, and Holy Spirit. It is an impossible mystery to explain, but it is confessed as true. All this is true through faith. I also learned when Christ comes into your life you will be transformed into a true human being. This is called sanctification. But it does not happen all at once. It takes place over your lifetime and involves a daily dying and a daily rising. This process is not complete until the believer arrives in heaven.

These were some of the basics. There is much in Christian theology that Christians would admit is mysterious and hard to understand. Most important is that though Jesus is the Messiah, he did not complete his work and will return at some unspecified time. This is called eschatology and apocalyptic. I should add my experience and knowledge of what it means to be Lutheran came through what is now the ELCA, the Evangelical Lutheran Church of America. Lutherans, like Jews, love to argue about who is "really" in the tradition. There are German Lutherans, Norwegian and Swedish and Finnish Lutherans, Missouri Synod Lutherans, and Wisconsin Synod Lutherans.

When my knowledge/study of the Holocaust and Judaism collided with Christian theology, there were problems that developed over time. Two of the problems proved to be unsolvable. First and foremost was the problem of anti-Judaism in Christian history and theology. Every year during what is called Holy Week, Christians tell the story of how Jesus came to be crucified. When they read out loud from the Gospel of John, it is "the Jews" that are pictured as the murderers. They are the ones who hand over or betray Jesus. They are the ones who want to see him crucified. They are the unbelievers. In John's Gospel it is "the Jews" who are called "children of the devil." Each Holy Week, sitting in Church and hearing these words, I would feel attacked.

But, since I was a teacher in the Lutheran church, I thought I could go out and teach pastors and laypeople about the potential toxic damage these New Testament texts could create. To my dismay, I discovered while my words received a polite reaction, it did not change what happened every Holy Week. The same story kept being read over and over. Pastors kept telling me they did not realize what they were reading and saying was so destructive. Conveniently not mentioned during most Sunday morning worship services was the fact that Jesus was Jewish. His disciples were Jewish. Yet anti-Judaism was so embedded within the Christian Scripture/tradition and story that it was endemic to the tradition. Over time, it became more and more difficult for me to attend church services.

And then I read about Nazi propaganda minister Goebbels, who had a radio program on Sunday mornings in which he loved to quote from the Gospel of John. He said, "Listen to what your own Lord says about the Jews." I had converted into a tradition that consciously or unconsciously, intentionally or unintentionally, promoted hatred of Jews. No matter how I tried to contextualize or rationalize some of the terrible New Testament texts, it did not work. And much to my shock, when I asked my freshmen religion students, "Who killed Jesus?," the vast majority answered, "the Jews." The real problem was not pastors being anti-Jewish and spreading lies about the Jews. The problem was that these texts and these ways of telling the Christian story were so much a part of Christian preaching and teaching that it was being communicated to people in the pews viscerally. Anti-Jewish teaching was entrenched within Christian history and tradition and could not be removed. I asked myself, "What are you doing in this tradition? How did you get here? How can you remain in such a community?"

A second issue related to the Holocaust. The Holocaust took place in the heart of Christian Europe, in a country which was half Roman Catholic and half Lutheran. I read everything I could and entered into the Holocaust as deeply as possible. I read everything Elie Wiesel wrote. I studied other books by survivors. I taught classes dealing with the Holocaust, entitled "After Auschwitz: The Holocaust and the Christian Faith." I immersed myself in films and online presentations. I traveled to Europe to see the camps, visiting Auschwitz/Birkenau, Buchenwald, and Theresienstadt. I spoke to Holocaust survivors. I came to realize that during the war, most Christians in Germany and the rest of Europe either collaborated

CHAPTER SIX: WHY GOD IS A PROBLEM

with the Nazis or were indifferent to what was happening to the Jews. During these years I took my students to listen to Holocaust survivors speak of what they had experienced in the camps. I was shocked and dismayed to hear the survivors' recollections. I concluded, after much soul-searching and grappling, that I could no longer, in good conscience, remain a Christian. I had to return to the Jewish community and tradition. This proved to be easier said than done.

I tried to discuss this predicament with my family, but it was difficult for them to understand. To them, especially my then wife, the Christian tradition was normative. It was all she knew. She could not imagine giving up that faith and she felt betrayed by my talk about leaving the church. In 1999 I traveled to Boston and met with Elie Wiesel, who encouraged me to continue to do what I must do. And through much wrestling and many, many literally sleepless nights, I decided the time had come. In the year 2000, I resigned my ordination and left the Christian church. The local Jewish congregation, Mount Zion, welcomed me back in their midst. I had returned home and at last could sleep in peace through the night.

There is one more important factor to understand about my return to Jewishness. I had returned to studying Jewish texts and traditions. As a part of my life at Augustana, I taught classes in Judaism. I learned and remembered the beauty and truth of my tradition and religion. I traveled to the State of Israel many times and felt safe and secure there. It felt like I was coming home, and it felt good and true. Wiesel was right. You cannot run away from who you are. "We do not begin to live our lives out of falsehood." It took me a long time to learn that truth and to live it out.

My immersion in Holocaust literature forced me to confront the horror of those days. And the more I confronted the horror, the more I wondered where God was during those days. It was then I realized the problem of God was not new. I had worked on the community lament psalms for my doctoral dissertation and thereafter lectured throughout the church on the importance of the laments in the biblical tradition. This melding or blending of anti-Judaism in Christian tradition, the lack of redemption in history despite the coming of the redeemer Jesus, the Holocaust writings of Elie Wiesel, the study of biblical and rabbinic lament traditions, and the beauty of Judaism over time coalesced in my mind to compel me to return to my Jewish roots.

Having said all of that, there is one thing about which it is important to be clear. Though Christian Scripture and tradition are anti-Judaism, individual Christians are not necessarily so. Many of the pastors and students I have met are not anti-Jewish or anti-Semitic. In fact, many Christians are shocked and dismayed to hear about their religious history, especially the Holocaust, regarding Jews. And my closest friends are Christian. That being said, the Christian tradition has come a ways since the Holocaust to rectify their relationship to the Jewish community. But it still has a ways to go.

Biography informs theology. This means while I imbibed much of Elie Wiesel's words, I was not Elie Wiesel. I had not lived through the Holocaust. I did not see what he saw. I did not experience what he experienced. But I did conclude his thinking on the justice of God to be on the mark. When I think of God, I find myself to be a religious skeptic. A part of my brain thinks, after the Holocaust, the notion of God no longer works. Another part of my brain hopes against hope there is a God with some sort of strange mysterious way of working in or interacting with our world. Despite my respect for the scholarship of the Jewish tradition, I have doubts about many of the interpretations of the traditional rabbis. They defended God when no real defense could work. In that way I am a modern American Jew who is proud to be Jewish but has doubts about the verity of the tradition.

There remains a question that haunts all of Wiesel's writings, as well as my own work on the laments. What good comes from questioning, accusing, or being angry at God? After such prayers are uttered, there is no response. You could just as well be talking to the wall or the ceiling. Undeserved suffering and evil seem to be doing quite well throughout human history. What is the point of wasting one's time screaming at the wind? As I noted earlier, a contemporary Reform rabbi, Harold Kushner, said "why" is the wrong question! We should ask, he says, "When suffering and

CHAPTER SIX: WHY GOD IS A PROBLEM

evil occur what should we do? We do not explain suffering or evil, we survive it." For Kushner, God may not be all-powerful. In every situation, God is doing what God can do to help us survive and thrive. And Kushner asks, "Can we forgive God for creating a world where the right thing does not always happen?"[1] This response is a popular version of what is called "process theology." I liked what Kushner was saying but his words seemed to diminish what we mean when we say the word *God*. And if, over the centuries, God has been influencing human beings, doing the best he can with people, there does not seem much or enough to show for it. If Kushner is right, then the activity and power of God has not been sufficiently efficient.

If we take the word *God* seriously, God has been and remains a problem. But what good does it do us to declare God a problem? It means those of us who have questions about the existence and justice of God are not crazy. God has always been problematic. If that is true, why did the ancients create the laments? Why does Wiesel believe, when it comes to God, the question is more important than the answer? Because the point of the laments is not only to convince God to act. The questions addressed to God are part of the inherent intimacy between God and God's people. The question assumes God is there; God cares, God wants to hear from us, and God is listening. The lament prayers create hope. Part of the covenant relationship God has with Israel includes being honest with each other. The laments come from a refusal to lie to God and a commitment to speak the truth to God. Such a relationship is built on love and justice! The ancients accepted the problematic light and darkness of God as part of any marriage, especially a marriage to God. In the Bible, when God was perceived as having acted according to the covenants, God was praised with plaudits, gratitude, and thanksgiving. When God forgave people their sins, God was heralded as one who rules out of God's inherent loving kindness. But when God was perceived as not acting justly, God was questioned and implored. This kind of intimacy is key to understanding the whole lament tradition as well as the writings of

1. Kushner, "When Bad Things Happen to Good People."

Elie Wiesel. When I myself pray, I embrace both questions, trust and hope against hope. I question God about his silence when suffering or evil happen. And I say the "Shema" ("Hear O' Israel, The Lord is God, The Lord is one") each morning and evening.

God has been a problem for as long as humans have worshiped the deity. God is and has always been invisible, inconsistent, ambiguous, unreliable, mysterious, and an enigma. Believing or trusting such a God has never been easy. We moderns with our skepticism and doubts are experiencing nothing new. This has been the predicament of religious believers over the centuries. Assuming I am right, why has faith in God endured? I suspect it is because the world seems more frightening without God than with God. And I think our human brains demand meaning and are reluctant to embrace absurdity. Beyond that I think people care about the truth. And they trust that indeed God is alive and still working in this world, hard as that may be to detect. Most believers are not deluded. They are aware that trusting in such a God is problematic, but they persevere nonetheless. Do they know they could be wrong? Yes! But they, like Wiesel, keep on keeping on despite the strangeness of God.

Judaism and the Problem of God

How do Judaism and most Jews deal with the problem of God? There is an old Jewish saying, mentioned above, "If you want to know what someone believes, do not listen to the mouth, follow the feet." In Judaism, what you do is more important than what you believe. The secret to life resides in the doing. When Elie Wiesel was asked what he had to say about God at the end of his life, he asserted, "I do not know what God is doing, but I know what I must do." Wherever there was undeserved suffering and evil, he was compelled to do what he could do to stop it. The greatest sin in his mind was indifference. In Jewish tradition, the belief is that God has given the Jewish people God's Torah or teaching. The Torah tells us what it means to live a life of character and integrity. The purpose of the commandments of God is to keep us sane and

CHAPTER SIX: WHY GOD IS A PROBLEM

to avoid chaos. God may be problematic—granted! There is nothing we can do about that. But we humans are commanded to do what we can do to make the world as sane as possible. God may be a problem, but there is work to be done.

How this works itself out in real life is a valid concern. It is one thing to decide doing is more important than believing, but figuring out how to live this out in the modern world is not easy. Jews debate among themselves across the world, especially in the state of Israel, what it means to not be indifferent and to live lives of character and integrity. The fact is that some Jews have given up on God. Some secular Jews observe and some ignore the commandments as interpreted by the ancient rabbis, but remain proud Jews. Some of these Jews study the ancient texts as bastions of truth to be mined. Other Jews continue, as best they can, to observe the traditional commandments, some in an Orthodox manner, some in a Conservative way, and others in Reform or Reconstructionist approaches. Regardless, for most Jews, the doing is vital. Even if they do not believe in God, they continue to observe at least some of the commandments. As they live their lives from day to day many try to live as a mensch, a person of honor and integrity. Many try to do acts of goodness called Mitzvot. They do not always succeed. Some Jews give in to temptation, egotism, and the appetites. But most struggle not to give in to indifference.

This is all well and good, but it does not solve the problem of God. How and why does a Jew live out the commandments when he or she does not believe there is a commander? This is a fine question that can only be answered by the fact that some Jews are committed to being Jews, God notwithstanding. I know that does not make any sense, but such is the situation. Maybe these Jews are saying by their lives, if Judaism is not the truth, it ought to be. Perhaps, in the end, it is better to say God will always be a problem and that is part of being God. When Jews do theology (talk about God) they do so in the service of the commandments and not for the sake of strengthening faith. Whether you believe or do not believe, God is a problem. As is often asserted, you cannot prove there is a God, and you cannot prove God does not exist.

83

The question is: what is the truth, what should you believe, and how should you live out your life?

Such is the predicament of the modern Jew trying to be honest and stay sane.

If we are to take Wiesel seriously, what are the implications for the way any of us live out our lives?

Chapter Seven: *How Should We Live after Auschwitz?*

For so many years I have been asking myself what it means for me, as a Jew, to live with a problematic God after Auschwitz. I have close friends who assure me there is no god. And I have other friends who tell me the problem is not God, it is human beings. And still others say God is a mystery whom we will never understand and ought not question. But I cannot forget listening to Holocaust survivors speaking about what it was like late at night in the camps, hearing people screaming from the gas chambers their prayers and confessing their faith to God: "God, I believe in you, I'm a religious man." "God, where are you?" They testify to hearing people praying the Shema (Jewish daily prayer) and singing the *Hatikvah* (what would become the Israeli national anthem) from within the gas chambers. The survivors tell us these are sounds a person cannot forget.

In this chapter I would like to face, as honestly as possible, the problem of God and its implications for the way we ought to live our lives. The fact is: As far as I can see, God is going to remain a problem, a mystery, and an enigma. The monotheistic religions each have their own revelations. At points they agree and at significant other points they disagree. But everyone who opens his or her eyes is caught in this dilemma and with these questions: What does it mean that I am here for a short time on the earth? How shall I live my life while I am here? And what does any of that have to do with God? Is there a God? Is there an afterlife? Is any of it true? Is there any sense in the chaos? How do we go on from day to day?

Below are eight points of reflection that might help your thinking about God. They have helped me.

1. *You are not crazy.* For the sake of our own sanity, we need to hear we are not crazy when we conclude God is a problem. Atheists from Marx to Freud to Nietzsche, each in their own way, have asserted the logic of atheism, although their writings say nothing new to religious believers. People who are honest and religious know God has always been a problem. And yes, contemporary American culture has raised questions about the existence of God. On the other hand, when we observe or listen to religious believers who are optimistic or confident in God's plans and purposes, we may think, "Are they crazy or am I crazy?" The true believers of atheism and theism have made and will continue to make their assertions, but I think Elie Wiesel would disagree with them. The great strength of Wiesel is his refusal to lie about what is happening in front of his and our eyes. Wiesel was determined to face the world as it is and not as we wish it to be. And for Wiesel, the biblical stories and the history of Jewish tradition encourage us to speak with honesty about and to God. Wiesel would not have us lie to defend, mollify, or appease God. And Wiesel believed God is not threatened by our questions, anger, accusations, or arguments. Our prayers to a problematic God must be honest and done with integrity.[1]

2. *Indifference is inhuman.* The problem of God ought not cause us to ignore or downplay the problem of human nature and human evil. Our religious traditions teach us not to stand idly by, never to be indifferent, to do whatever we

---

1. For an important lament after the Holocaust, see Isaac Bashevis Singer's "Untitled (Treatise to God)."

CHAPTER SEVEN: HOW SHOULD WE LIVE AFTER AUSCHWITZ?

can in every situation to make the world a saner place. The silence of God does not disqualify the need for us to act as well as human beings can act. For Wiesel, indifference is decadence. As he has said, a person who is indifferent is dead but he or she doesn't know it yet.[2]

The religious traditions of the three major monotheisms urge their followers to not be indifferent. But, what specifically does it mean to not be indifferent? For Wiesel, to be a human being is to care about the other person. It means if you see someone suffering evil and you can do something to help, you must do what you can do. It means to be a human being is to not look away, but try to help. Sometimes there will not be much you can do. Wiesel would assert, "I don't know what you can do, say a prayer, write a letter, shed a tear. There is so much in this world that should move us."[3] In his book, *The Town Beyond the Wall*, Wiesel pictures a Holocaust survivor returning to his hometown to confront "the man in the window." When the Nazis were rounding up the Jews in Wiesel's town, and Jewish men women and children were forced to stand under the hot sun for hours upon hours, the children were begging for water. The survivor remembers looking up at the man in the window, who saw what was happening below, but closed his window shades and remained indifferent. In the book, the survivor, Michael, says to his friend Pedro, "Do you understand that I need to understand? To understand the Others, those who watched us depart for the unknown; those who observed us, without emotion, while we became objects—living sticks of wood—and carefully numbered victims." Michael goes on,

> This is the thing I had wanted to understand, ever since the war: how can a human being remain indifferent? The executioners I understood, also the victims, though with more difficulty. But the others, all the others, those who were neither for or against, those who sprawled in

2. Wiesel, Augustana Lecture.
3. Wiesel, Augustana Lecture.

passive patience, those who told themselves, "The storm will blow over and everything will be normal again," those who thought themselves above the battle, those who were permanently mere spectators—all those were closed to me, incomprehensible.[4]

Michael recalls the man in the window.

It was then that I saw him. A face in the window across the way. The curtains hid the rest of him; only his head was visible. It was like a balloon. Bald, flat nose. Wide empty eyes. A bland face, banal, bored: no passion ruffled it. I watched it for a long time. It was gazing out, reflecting no pity, no pleasure, no shock, not even anger or interest. Impassive, cold, impersonal. The face was indifferent to the spectacle.[5]

Again, Michael says,

The third in the triangle. Between victims and executioners there is a mysterious bond; they belong to the same universe; one is the negation of the other. The German's logic was clear, comprehensible to the victims. Even evil and madness show a stunted intelligence. But this was not true of the other. The spectator is entirely beyond us. He sees without being seen. He is there but unnoticed. The footlights hide him. He neither applauds nor hisses; his presence is evasive and commits him less than his absence might. He says nothing. He is there, but he acts as if he were not. Worse: he acts as if the rest of us were not.[6]

In the *The Town Beyond the Wall*, Michael finally travels to his hometown and confronts the face in the window:

"Coward!" I shouted, and crashed my fist down on the table. "You're a shameful coward! You haven't got the courage to do either good or evil! The role of spectator suited you to perfection. They killed? You had nothing to do with it. Your conscience is clear. 'Not guilty, your

---

4. Wiesel, *Town Beyond the Wall*, 148–49.
5. Wiesel, *Town Beyond the Wall*, 150.
6. Wiesel, *Town Beyond the Wall*, 151.

CHAPTER SEVEN: HOW SHOULD WE LIVE AFTER AUSCHWITZ?

honor!' You're a disgusting coward! You hedge; you want to be on the winning side no matter what! It's easy to say, 'I am I and they are they and to hell with them!'" The face in the window finally speaks, "You hate me, don't you?" Michael answers, "No." I said, "I don't hate you." "I feel contempt for you. That's worse. The man who inspires hatred is still human; but not the man who inspires contempt. You don't feel contempt for the executioner; you hate him, and you want him dead. You feel contempt only for cowards. People like you retreat to an ivory tower and say to themselves, 'All the world's a stage and all the men and women merely players. Ah, how pleasant when they make us shiver!' Hatred implies humanity: it has its coordinates, its motifs, its themes, its harmonics. Under certain conditions it can elevate men. But contempt has only one implication: decadence."[7]

Wiesel comments, "The spectator has nothing of the human in him: he is a stone in the street, the cadaver of an animal, a pile of dead wood. He is there, he survives us, he is immobile. The spectator reduces himself to the level of an object. He is no longer he, you or I: he is 'it.'"[8]

For Wiesel, evil is real. And he believes human beings have the capacity to do good and the capacity to do evil. He asserts that when we encounter evil, we have a moral responsibility to do what we can do to oppose that evil.

3. *You cannot save the world.* There are many things wrong with the world. You will not be able to fix everything or everyone who is sick, wrong, or evil. Some people and some situations are so broken they cannot be fixed, or you cannot conceive of what you can do to help. But wherever you live, you can find something you can do. Wiesel held, and I agree, that for human beings to be human they must care for their fellow humans. And caring can take all sorts of shapes and styles. For one person it may take the shape of

---

7. Wiesel, *Town Beyond the Wall*, 159.
8. Wiesel, *Town Beyond the Wall*, 160.

marching in protest, for another it will be writing a letter, for another helping someone get to the hospital, for still another stopping to have a conversation with a lonely person. Caring can be doing something small or large, depending on your ability. And people will disagree on exactly what should be done. But the key is to do something, even if it is a small thing, do something to help.

In the Christian New Testament, there is the story of the Good Samaritan who happens upon the wounded man and is compelled to act. Throughout the Quran, Muslims are encouraged to resist indifference and care for the neighbor in pain. And then this great quote from Wiesel:

> True, we are often too weak to stop injustices; but the least we can do is to protest against them. True, we are too poor to eliminate hunger; but in feeding one child, we protest against hunger. True, we are too timid and powerless to take on all the guards of all the political prisons in the world; but in offering our solidarity to one prisoner we denounce all the tormentors. True, we are powerless against death; but as long as we help one man, one woman, one child live one hour longer in safety and dignity, we affirm man's right to live.[9]

When asked what we can do in the presence of burning children, Wiesel responded, "Try to save one child."[10]

4. *Hope, faith, and reason.* Believing in God is not realistic or intelligible. God is a problem. God, if God exists and if our expectations of what it means to be God are realistic, is inconsistent, ambiguous, unreliable, and silent. I am not so much a person of faith. I am a person of hope. Faith is trusting in God without knowing for sure. Faith and hope are not the same thing. Faith comes from a deep commitment to trust despite what a person sees with their eyes. Hope, on the other hand, is an elusive, improbable, wishful, uncertain

---

9. Wiesel, Augustana Lecture.
10. Wiesel, Augustana Lecture.

CHAPTER SEVEN: HOW SHOULD WE LIVE AFTER AUSCHWITZ?

desire or yearning. And I find myself lying awake in the middle of the night, employing my reason to figure out what is true, thinking about such things. The facts seem clear to our reason: when we die, we will disappear into the ether, as with anesthesia in the hospital, except we will go to sleep and not wake up. That is what my reason tells me. Reason tells me there is no God, no afterlife, no purpose or meaning to our lives. We are here for a while depending on the luck of our genetic background and our fortuitous avoidance of accidents. And then we disappear. On the other hand, my fragile hope tells me something is going on and there may or may not be a God at work in the universe. My hope is there is something going on and I hope there is a life after life. And I hope despite all the evil in the world I can observe, that there yet remains a God at work in the universe. Perhaps because I am a religious romantic attracted to hope. I want there to be a God, but I doubt there is one. I want there to be an ultimate justice brought to us by a Messiah, but I doubt it will ever happen. I want there to be a plan or purpose for our existence in human history, but I doubt there is one.

I think we should try to be as honest as we can when it comes to God. I, like you, can be envious of those with a simplistic faith or lack of faith in God. It is not so simple for me. In the shadow of the Holocaust and other life-taking catastrophes, a simplistic faith is naïve and dishonest. A hope against hope is understandable if not defensible. We know it does not make sense and yet we hope.

Some years ago, I spoke in a small Minnesota town, and after my lecture a woman asked me if I knew before I left town I would be dying, would I believe I would go to heaven? I answered: "I do not believe so, but I hope it is true." I suspect this is the situation for most of us. We were brought up on the biblical stories. We attended synagogue, church, or mosque regularly. But as we have gotten older and wiser, we are not sure any of it is true. We can pretend earlier generations had it easier, believed with a stronger if more naïve faith, but we would be wrong. God has always been a problem and people have had to live with that unsolved problem. They may not have articulated it with clarity but that was their existential predicament, as it is ours. We are eternally caught in the perplexing, inevitable tension between what we can discern with our reason, what we believe, and what we hope is true.

5. *Courage and Cowardice.* Courage is the ability to act despite fear and cowardice is the refusal to act because of fear. Wiesel believes human beings have the capacity to act well and the capacity to act poorly. And that seems to be true. We humans are as inconsistent, ambiguous, unreliable, and mysterious as God. We have moral capacities according to which we sometimes act. But we also have the capacity to ignore our moral instincts. We have the capacity to be cowardly and the capacity to be courageous. We have the capacity to be evil. There is a great quote from the prolific writer Joseph Epstein about the choices we make in our lives:

> We do not choose to be born. We do not choose our parents. We do not choose our historical epoch, or the country of our birth, or the immediate circumstances of our upbringing. We do not, most of us, choose to die; nor do we choose the time or conditions of our death. But within all this realm of choicelessness, we do choose how we shall live: courageously or in cowardice, honorably or dishonorably, with purpose or adrift. We decide what is important and what is trivial in life. We decide that what makes us significant is either what we do or what we refuse to do. But no matter how indifferent the universe may be to our choices and decisions, these choices and decisions are ours to make. We decide. We choose. And as we decide and choose, so are our lives formed.[11]

Most of us will have moments in our lives when we are called upon to act courageously. It will not be easy. We may be afraid. The key, so far as I can see, is to act despite our fear.

---

11. Epstein, *Ambition*, 298.

6. *Covenants and a problematic God.* Assuming we are correct in asserting God is a problem, what, if anything, is it fair to expect from God? Would we be wise to have low or no expectations? Are we merely deluded in expecting God to act? If God is a problem, is God a problem we will never be able to solve? Are we to be left with only a few vague and elusive vectors? What, after all, can we trust when it comes to God?

We can trust that trusting will not be easy. And we can trust this God knows trusting is a spiritual struggle. In a chaotic world such as we live in, trusting or expecting things from God is a precarious process. On the other hand, not having any expectations creates its own problems. God may be at work on our planet, but God's methodology or process is problematic at best, and we are better off being honest about that! It is not our job to defend and apologize for God. Our job, in a world after Auschwitz, is to be as honest as we can about the character of God.

This raises the question of covenants. After Auschwitz, what are we to make of *covenants* between God and the Jewish people? Where did they originate? Were they just something invented? Do they have any power?

Traditionally, covenants have been defined as, "The people Israel would be faithful to God, as evidenced by the observance of the commandments, and God in turn would protect and preserve Israel."[12] "The covenant is an expression of moral coherence: the idea that the universe is not completely random, an agglomeration of events without meaning or justice. A covenant represents the reassurance that the world does have a larger structure, a framework of meaning."[13] And that is precisely the problem with God after the Holocaust. Israel, the people of God, were murdered at the rate of ten thousand a day in the Nazi camps. Between 1939 and 1945 a million and a half children under the age of ten were killed. Whatever the covenants of old meant, after

---

12. Tuling, *Thinking about God*, 276.
13. Tuling, *Thinking about God*, 278.

the Holocaust they need to be reinterpreted. But what can we reinterpret within our covenants and yet remain faithful to their power? What can we say about the covenants? Did they come from God as a revelation or were they created by ingenious, imaginative religious writers? After all, what is a covenant? It is a sacred pledge, a vow, a promise, a commitment between God and human beings. Between humans covenants can and are sometimes broken. Is the same true for divine covenants? The biblical covenants bind God to Israel. But do they bind God? Do they bind human beings? Covenants are vital for trusting or deciding not to trust God. If you continue to believe in the existence, purposes, and meaning of someone called God despite Auschwitz, it must be because you keep hoping against hope and logic that the covenants remain and are valid. It is fair to say though God be faithless, some Jews will remain faithful! But how do these Jews know or think or believe there is a God out there, up there, or even in here, to be faithless? They trusted in the covenants, God's word that God could be trusted. They believed God was for them and not against them. They knew God was problematic because they saw with clear eyes what was happening in front of them and yet, despite, in spite, and to spite they kept on believing. The silence of God could not deter them. What are we to make of such faith? Does it reflect a naïve, fearful, unintelligent, ridiculous trust? Or is such faith to be lauded as a sign of determined religious integrity in the face of monstrous evil? Or is it the kind of faith that is meant to hold back fear and reassure the child in each of us? We want to believe that ultimately good will vanquish evil and joy will defeat sadness. We want to witness the victory of faith and prayer over terror and cruelty. When all is said and done, for some Jews covenants have to do with memory. If we will remember the promises made by God so long ago, if we will remember who we are and where we came from, then and only then, we will be able to survive. Jewish

CHAPTER SEVEN: HOW SHOULD WE LIVE AFTER AUSCHWITZ?

existence and survival are tied to the ancient covenants. As Wiesel often said, "In memory lies redemption."

7. *"And God in all this?"* Uri Zvi Grinberg has written a poem entitled "They have Killed Their God?" The poem describes the appearance of Jesus in a small village somewhere in Eastern Europe in those days. He is looking for his brothers—he is looking for his people. When he does not find them, he asks a passerby, "Where are the Jews?" "Killed," says the passerby. "All of them?" "All of them." "And their homes?" "Demolished." "Their synagogues?" "Burned." "Their sages?" "Dead." "Their students?" "Dead too." "And their children? What about their children?" "Dead too, all of them, they are all dead." And Jesus begins to weep over the slaughter of his people. He weeps so hard that people turn around to look at him, and suddenly one peasant exclaims, "Hey, look at that, here is another Jew, how did he stay alive?" "And the peasants throw themselves on Jesus and kill him too, killing their God, thinking they are killing just another Jew."[14]

The question of God must and will remain a question. Those who are sure they know do not know. Whatever we mean by the word *God* is weighted down with all sorts of theodicies, philosophical speculations, theological rationalizations, imagination, and wishful thinking. If you study the Jewish, Christian, and Islamic Scriptures you will find despite all the flowery language thrown toward and about God, the methodology of God remains a problem. Be careful of those who are too sure there is a God and those too sure there is no God. There is no way to prove either assertion. God remains a mystery. Saying this is not a cop-out; it is not a matter of blind faith. Believers are not trying to deny the truth and facts about God. It is rather a determination to be honest about the problematics of God in the face of Auschwitz.

8. *Being a community of yearners.* Many years ago, our university religion department interviewed candidates for a

14. Wiesel, *A Jew Today*, 182–83.

position in theology. When we asked one of the interviewees to explain her religious attitude toward God, she told us, "I am a yearner." I find this description quite apt for our contemporary situation regarding God. For those of us who are religious, our hope is there is a God who, with moral and just purpose and planning, is working in the universe. These words express our yearning for it to be true. We are not sure any of it is true, but we yearn for it to be true. We know we could be wrong, but we are a community of yearners, hoping against hope it is true. We are aware we could be wrong, but we yearn to be right.

You may be wondering what Christians have thought and written about the problem of God. Of course, over the last two thousand years much has been written and spoken. I have been particularly impressed by this one puzzling reflection: During World War II, Dietrich Bonhoeffer, a Lutheran pastor in Germany, was arrested by the Nazis. While in prison he wrote many letters in which he wrestled with what it meant to be Christian in the modern world. One of the most intriguing and confusing insights he wrote about was his idea that as contemporary Christians we are compelled to live in a world without God before God.[15]

> We cannot be honest unless we recognize that we have to live in the world *etsi deus non daretur* [without God, before God]. And this is just what we do recognize—before God! God himself compels us to recognize it. So our coming of age leads us to a true recognition of our situation before God. God would have us know that we must live as men who manage our lives without him. The God who is with us is the God who forsakes us (Mark 15:34). The God who lets us live in the world without the working hypothesis of God is the God before whom we stand continually. Before God and with God we live without God. God lets himself be pushed out of the world on to the cross. He is weak and powerless in the world, and that is precisely the way, the only way, in which he is with us

---

15. Bonhoeffer, *Letters and Papers from Prison*, 359–361.

CHAPTER SEVEN: HOW SHOULD WE LIVE AFTER AUSCHWITZ?

and helps us. Matt. 8:17 makes it quite clear that Christ helps us, not by virtue of omnipotence, but by virtue of his weakness and suffering.[16]

Many scholars have tried to explain what Bonhoeffer meant with these words. I am not sure I can clearly decipher what he was saying, but his attempt is a good illustration of how Christians might respond to the problem of God. For some people Bonhoeffer sounds too vague, tentative, and ambiguous. I am unsure what Bonhoeffer meant and if what he meant makes any sense. What does impress me is his willingness to address the problem of God. We, who are alive at this time, are compelled to come to terms with a God who abandons us and yet remains God. How does that work?

The lament tradition in the Scriptures teaches us the importance of questioning an invisible, mysterious, and silent God. It teaches us to obey God's commandments, to not stand idly by while someone is suffering, and to do this even as we are not sure God is obligated to adhere to the same commandments and even if we are not sure God has not remained indifferent to human pain and suffering.

---

16. Bonhoeffer, *Letters and Papers from Prison*, 360–361.

Afterword

My experience as a Jew has been different than that of Elie Wiesel. While my parents were survivors of the Holocaust, my eyes have not seen what Elie Wiesel's saw. And my understanding of God, though strongly influenced by Wiesel, is somewhat different. Having grown up in America, my views about God have been influenced by the secular, modern, scientific, and technological temper of the culture as well as the Jewish tradition. When I think about God, I have come to trust my common senses. I struggle to understand traditional Jewish perspectives on God. I wrestle with how to reconcile traditional Jewish commitments and beliefs about God and contemporary scientific perspectives on the nature of our universe. In many ways I am a religious skeptic who like David Hume is skeptical about skepticism. I do not trust my self-serving ability to think as a valid way to truth. Yet I am compelled to theologize and philosophize. Much as I am convinced I do not know what I am talking about, I believe I have a few ideas worth thinking over. Perhaps that is my goal: to make the reader rethink what he or she always thought was true.

In the end, I am a Jew who has spent much time among Christians, who learned their theological jargon but could not reconcile my soul to their message. I fear Christian tradition has lobbed so much nonsense on top of the poor shoulders of the man named Jesus. Believing him to be the Messiah, they declared

AFTERWORD

Jesus victorious over sin, death, and evil, and decided to ignore that fact that sin, death, and evil are still doing very well. And many are convinced he will return one day to complete his work. But more than any of that there lies in Christian Scripture a pervasive anti-Judaism that I could never tolerate.

The truth is that I am in love with and part of Jewish history and tradition and feel terrible guilt and shame for having left it for too long. The fact is I am also a religious romantic who likes to imagine I am not alone but am accompanied by unseen forces. But what is it about Judaism that specifically attracts me? In Christianity, the goal seems to be faith in the grace of God through Jesus Christ. God works in the individual to create faith. But in Judaism what you do determines who you are. Faith is the result of acting, not the other way around. In Judaism the key is to realize the importance of the question more than the answer to the question. Jews talk about faith and its importance, but Judaism as a religion embraces the questions that haunt you and the actions you do every day. The religion recognizes what we do not know and that attracts me. But Judaism is more than a religion. It is a tribal community, a nation of individuals inextricably connected to each other, some religious, others irreligious, connected to and sometimes critical of the State of Israel.

Jewish tradition teaches that wherever God is, that is where truth resides, and wherever truth is discovered that is where God resides. From day to day, I am less and less convinced what I can say about God or religion for sure. As Wiesel asserts,

> Of course, man must interrogate God, as did Abraham, articulate his anger, as did Moses; and shout his sorrow, as did Job. But only the Jew opts for Abraham—who questions—and for God who is questioned. He claims every role and assumes every destiny: he is both sum and synthesis. Only the Jew knows that he may oppose God as long as he does so in defense of His creation. God gave the law, but it is up to man to interpret it—and his interpretation is binding on God and commits him.[1]

1. Wiesel, *A Jew Today*, 6.

Perhaps the most difficult problem in trusting God is control. I must confess that sometimes when I say the word *God*, I wonder if I am talking about a combination of the tooth fairy, Santa Claus, and the Easter bunny. Is there such a force as God in the universe? My uncertainty is obsessive. We humans need control and meaning to live our lives well. Our religions tell us God is in control. They say, God created us and gives meaning to our existence. If God exists, then God has the power and control to do as God wants to do. But if there is no God, then we exist in a universe that has order and chaos mingled and we are left to do the best we can. Either way I am not sure I have much control of what happens to me day by day. To say God is driving the bus, that God is in control, defies what we mean by control. The world seems to be out of control. The Holocaust, wars, pandemics, horrific acts of nature and man seem to happen without anyone in control. If God is in control, I am not sure what the word *control* means. And I am not sure I am willing to cede control to a deity that seems so inconsistent. Now some would say, "God's ways are mysterious, and we are not able to understand them." But what is there to understand? During the Holocaust, a million and a half Jewish children under the age of ten were exterminated. What is there to understand? If you tell me it is all part of God's plan, why would I want to believe in a God who would, as part of some bizarre plan, kill a million children? That God would be evil.

Our real problem is that our sophisticated, intelligent mammalian brains need to feel control and meaning to survive well. Our brains are amazingly agile yet vulnerably fragile. When we feel out of control and when we can see no meaning in what is happening, we do not function well. We can and do try to create control and meaning, and sometimes that works. We can and do tolerate an amazing amount of chaos, but there are limits. When chaos becomes cumulative and overwhelms us, we may not function rationally. And it may be that when the craziness of chaos comes close to us, we less desire theological explanation or laments and more consolation and comfort. And God in all of this? The best we can

AFTERWORD

say, though awfully vague, is that God is at work fighting against chaos. How God is at work is problematic and mysterious.

But why do I, a Jew, continue to hope there is a God at work in our world despite all the questions, doubts, and problems? It finally comes down to this: when the big bang happened, why was there anything to go bang? Where did the material come from for there to be a big bang? I cannot conceive of our entire solar system existing without a cause. While I am aware that we invented the word *God*, I am not sure the cause was God, but I cannot rule that possibility out. And what do I mean by the word *God*? Is it a powerful force? Does it have spiritual power? What does the word *God* have to do with the Jewish, Christian, or Muslim understandings of God? In other words, I am not sure there is a God, but I am not convinced there is not a God, creator, or first cause. Is that enough to latch on to one's need for control and meaning? Probably not! But it is what we have, and we ought to be honest about it.

Yet, here is the real problem of talking about God in our time. The metaphysic has collapsed. By metaphysic I mean a picture or story of the way the universe works. We no longer buy into the notion of a three-story universe, with God above us in heaven, and sinners below us in hell. We have learned about the vast expanse of space, watched men land on our moon, seen our scientists building spaceships to go to Mars, and we are living through the Covid pandemic; the old story no longer works for many of us. The old metaphysic has died. Of course, I am not saying anything new. We have known this for hundreds of years. Talking about or to God is problematic! And yet there remain those who believe, "God is God, and His ways are sometimes incomprehensible—and so they must be. If you could always understand what He is doing, He would not be what He is, you would not be what you are."[2] I love these words, their romance, passion, and hope. It makes me want to believe and trust and yet my brain shaped by modernity finds it hard to trust, hard to believe. I'm sorry, but too much craziness has happened in our world to be naïve about someone called God.

2. Wiesel, *A Jew Today*, 70.

REFLECTIONS OF AN UNCONVERTED CONVERT

Assuming God is a problem, can this problem be solved? Elie Wiesel helps us. For Wiesel, God is a puzzling mystery and a problem. God's silence during the Holocaust remains inexplicable. But Wiesel does not dwell on this enigma. His response is to say, I do not know what God is doing. But I know what I must do. For Wiesel, the problem of the inactivity of God means he, Wiesel, needs to do what he can to stand with the neighbor in pain. Throughout his life he traveled across the world, wherever people were being oppressed, to do what he could do to bring attention to their plight, to call out evil, to give comfort to the suffering, and thereby to refuse to be indifferent.

Wiesel teaches us:

> For in our tradition, celebration of life is more important than mourning over the dead. When a wedding procession encounters a funeral procession in the street, the mourners must halt to allow the wedding party to proceed. In more general terms, Judaism teaches man to overcome despair. What is Jewish history if not an endless quarrel with God? And as in every love affair, there are quarrels and reconciliations, more quarrels, and more reconciliations. And yet neither God nor the Jews ever gave up on the other. There were many periods in our past when we had every right in the world to turn to God and say, "Enough. Since You seem to approve of all these persecutions, all these outrages, have it Your way: let Your world go on without Jews. Either You are our partner in history or You are not. If You are, do Your share; if You are not, we consider ourselves free of past commitments. Since You choose to break the Covenant, so be it." And yet, and yet. We went on believing, hoping, invoking His name. In the endless engagement with God, we proved to Him that we were more patient than He, more compassionate too. In other words, we did not give up on Him either. For this is the essence of being Jewish, never to give up—never to yield to despair.[3]

---

3. Wiesel, *A Jew Today*, 163–64.

AFTERWORD

Think That You May Be Wrong

But what if I'm wrong? During the many years I taught religion at Augustana University, I had a sign on my door that read: "Think that you may be wrong." I suspect my students assumed this sign was intended for them. While that is partially true, the sign was more so intended for me to remember I could be wrong. So, after writing this book I am asking myself, where could I be wrong?

I have asserted my hope against hope that God exists. I could be wrong and there may be no God in the universe, only our own isolated blue planet. I know this and accept the risk of being wrong. I could be engaged in wishful thinking. The problem is a collision of metaphysics in our brains. Those of us who are religious and want to believe there is a God are also influenced and shaped by the scientific, technological, secular mindset. This collision of ways of looking at the universe makes it difficult to trust completely in either metaphysic.

As to the laments, I understand their minority status within Jewish and Christian traditions. Questioning and accusing God of wrongdoing sounds like a lack of faith and trust in the divine management of the universe. Perhaps it is ludicrous to question and yell at God when there is no response. I suspect the ancient rabbis knew about the lament tradition but decided to downplay it for the sake of maintaining laypeople's trust in God. And perhaps I have overemphasized the importance of arguing with God in Jewish tradition. But after the Holocaust I cannot see how anyone who has looked at what happened during those years would not stop and ask questions about the character and morality of God. I know the synagogue, the church, and the mosque seem to have lost the importance of the interrogative within their respective traditions, especially in public worship. The questioning of God from within faith seems to have been abandoned. But I do recognize that when we say the word *God*, it comes with certain expectations filled with all sorts of theological presuppositions and interpretations. Maybe it is true that God operates in the world in ways we cannot comprehend. The mystery defense of God is convincing, though it sounds to me like a cop-out. To me it seems like a way of not dealing seriously with what is happening in front of our eyes. As to the atheists in our days, their arguments are not new, yet they may be right.

After I returned to the Jewish tradition in the year 2000, a student stopped by my university office and asked me this question: "Dr. Haar, have you ever thought you were making a mistake by leaving the Christian church?" Her question was about the truth of Christianity. The student was asking me if it had occurred to me that I could be wrong. But for me, leaving the church was less about the falsity or truth of the Christian faith and more about not running away from myself. You cannot be who you are not. No matter how hard I tried to be a Christian, and I worked diligently at it, I could not constitutionally achieve it. Anyone who listened to me during my Christian years would have concluded, "He is really Jewish." Wiesel was right. I could not and cannot live out my life through falsehood. Does that mean I think Judaism is right and Christianity is wrong? No, I think when it comes to the truth about God, the Christian "yes" and the Jewish "no," with regard to the truth, are both vital and appropriate. Each tradition keeps the other tradition honest. Christians claim sin, death, and evil have been defeated by the cross and resurrection of Jesus, whom they call the Christ or Messiah. Jews dispute this claim because when they look at the world they see, sin, death, and evil flourishing, Jesus notwithstanding. Muslims think Jesus is the Christ, but they do not believe he died on the cross. These traditions would be considerably more honest if they would each admit they could be wrong. I doubt this will happen very soon. But we all can realize, can we not, that religious traditions are only glimpses of the truth? If theologians and religious functionaries from each religion could each admit how tentative and ambiguous their beliefs are, they would keep their members considerably saner, less judgmental, and free to question the justice of God.

I had a close friend, a Lutheran pastor, who listened carefully and with concern to my reservations about Christian anti-Judaism. She tried to understand how the Christian story inevitably attacks Jews and Judaism. She wanted to get it, to sympathize, to empathize

AFTERWORD

with me, her friend. A few weeks later, I heard her preach about the hypocrisy and cowardice of the Pharisees. Later that day when we had lunch, I pointed out to her what she had done. She was shocked at how she could have missed what she was saying. And she asserted, "If you were not standing beside me to call me out, I would not have been able to hear what I was saying." And therein lies the problem. For the past two thousand years when Christians have told the story of Jesus, they have implicitly and sometimes explicitly been attacking Jews and Judaism. This pastor then said, "If I missed what I was saying, how many other pastors and priests are not able to hear what they are saying?" Anti-Judaism is embedded within the Christian story. When Christians tell the story of Jesus, they emphasize continuity and discontinuity with their Jewish roots. Christians employ the Jewish Scriptures, refer to Jesus as a rabbi, and on good days recognize that Jesus was Jewish and not Christian. But Christian tradition has been upset by the Jewish refusal to accept Jesus as the Christ. And their Gospels, John in particular, function to subvert what we call Judaism today.

This book is about responsibility, the failure of God's responsibility and the failure of Christian or human responsibility.[4] After the Holocaust Christians and Jews have come a ways but we have a long way to go. The Christian story is so toxic and infected I am not sure how it can be fixed. But there are a few Christians who are trying to alert their listeners to the problem. And we should be clear, not all Christians are anti-Jewish and not all of Christianity is toxic, yet within the soul of the Christian tradition lies a toxic stream of anti-Judaism.

---

4. See the recent book by Dara Horn, *People Love Dead Jews*, 190–91.

Bibliography

Bonhoeffer, Dietrich. *Letters and Papers from Prison.* Enlarged ed. Edited by Eberhard Bethge. New York: Macmillan, 1972.
Epstein, Joseph. *Ambition: The Secret Passion.* New York: E. P. Dutton, 1980.
Haar, Murray J. "The God-Israel Relationship in the Community Lament Psalms." PhD diss., Union Theological Seminary, 1985.
———. "Job After Auschwitz." *Interpretation* (July 1999) 265–75.
Horn, Dara, *People Love Dead Jews.* New York: W. W. Norton, 2021.
Kushner, Harold. "When Bad Things Happen to Good People." YouTube. https://www.youtube.com/watch?v=AKx-iJG5qrE.
Laytner, Anson. *Arguing with God.* Northvale, NJ: Jason Aronson, 1990.
Luhrmann, T. M. *How God Becomes Real.* Princeton: Princeton University Press, 2020.
Oz, Amos, and Fania Oz-Salzberger. *jews and words.* New Haven: Yale University Press, 2012.
Singer, Isaac Bashevis. "Untitled (Treatise to God)." *Tablet Daily Online Magazine,* fragments, date unknown. Copyright 2021 by the Isaac Bashevis Singer Literary Trust.
Tuling, Kari H. *Thinking about God.* Philadelphia: Jewish Publication Society, 2020.
Wiesel, Elie. *A Jew Today.* New York: Random House, 1978.
———. *All Rivers Run to the Sea.* New York: Alfred A. Knopf, 1995.
———. *And the Sea Is Never Full.* New York: Alfred A. Knopf, 1999.
———. *Ani Maamin.* New York: Schocken, 1995.
———. *Augustana Lecture.* Augustana College, Sioux Falls, SD, November, 1979.
———. *Legends of Our Time.* New York: Schocken, 1982.
———. *Night.* New York: Hill and Wang, 1958.
———. *The Town Beyond the Wall.* New York: Schocken, 1982.
———. *The Trial of God.* New York: Random House, 1979.